BETWEEN WORLDS

the publishing CIRCLE™

Send permission requests to the publisher at:
admin@thepublishingcircle.com.
Attention: Permissions Coordinator
Regarding Inga Aksamit

DISCLAIMER: The Publisher and the Author make no representations or warranties with respect to the accuracy or completeness of the contents of this work and specifically disclaim all warranties, including without limitations, warranties of fitness for a particular purpose. No warranty may be created or extended by sales or promotional materials. The advice and strategies contained herein may not be suitable for every situation. This work is sold with the understanding that the Publisher is not engaged in rendering medical, legal, accounting, or other professional services. If professional assistance is required, the services of a competent professional person should be sought. Neither the Publisher nor the Author shall be liable for damages arising here from.

The fact that an organization or website is referred to in this work as a citation and/or a potential source of further information does not mean that the Author or Publisher endorses the information the organization or website may provide or recommendations it may make. Further, readers should be aware that Internet websites listed in this work may have changed or disappeared between when this work was written and when it is read. The Publisher is not responsible for the Author's website, other mentioned websites, or content of any website that is not owned by the publisher.

The names of some individuals referenced in this book have been changed to protect and honor their privacy.

All content is the Author's opinion only.

BETWEEN WORLDS: AN EXPAT'S QUEST FOR BELONGING
FIRST EDITION
ISBN 978-1-955018-87-6 (PAPERBACK)
ISBN 978-1-955018-85-2 (LARGE-PRINT PAPERBACK)
ISBN 978-1-955018-76-0 (HARDCOVER)
ISBN 978-1-955018-77-7 (E-BOOK)

Cover and book design by Michele Uplinger

Between Worlds

An Expat's Quest for Belonging

a memoir

INGA AKSAMIT

"Aksamit's intelligence, curiosity, and commitment to exploring the prism of her peripatetic life, while honoring the incredible foundation of love her parents gave her, make for an engaging read. By the end it is a profound and moving expression of an extraordinary life that has been fully lived and understood. The memoir tells a vivid story that comes to a very satisfying conclusion."

LISA LIANG
CREATOR OF *Alien Citizen: An Earth Odyssey*

"An "aha" moment for travel addicts and "rootless" passport holders, Inga's story brings this subculture experience to the limelight as she threads her story via her unlikely globetrotting childhood and jarring personal experiences wrought from her family's flights from violent international conflicts. If you enjoy living on the edge, "Between Worlds" will bring you to it—and back."

JANIS COUVREUX
AUTHOR OF *Sail Cowabunga!: A Family's Ten Years at Sea*

"If you have ever lived in between cultures and felt misunderstood by others around you, this book is for you. Inga Aksamit's memoir takes us on her personal journey of growing up in different countries and her search for belonging. Her story resonates with many Third Culture Kids who try to make sense of their upbringing and how it has shaped them today. Beautifully written, and raw to the complexities of navigating a globally mobile life. A must read!"

MARIE SUAZO
AUTHOR OF *Tales of a Diplomat's Daughter*

"Between Worlds takes the reader on a tour of Inga Aksamit's remarkable life involving, among many other things, a series of evacuations from war zones, and a bewildering succession of new schools where Inga is always the new girl. Displaying an unfailing openness to other cultures and with the support of her loving and resourceful parents, Inga seems to have emerged unscathed from all this and it is only in a moving section towards the end of the book that Inga and the reader discover the hidden traumas that her unconventional upbringing has left her with. A fascinating read."

DAVID GRAY
AUTHOR OF *Words from a Wild Place: A Borneo Journal*

Dedication

To my parents,
Carroll E. Aksamit and Dorothy Aksamit,
who dreamed of a life of adventure
and made it all possible.

Acknowledgments

I owe deep gratitude to my critique partners from Redwood Writers in Santa Rosa, Marilyn Lanier and Henri Bensussen, for dedicating countless hours to reviewing my manuscript chapter by chapter, including every painstaking rewrite. They relentlessly slashed exclamation points, run-on sentences, and cliches with their digital sickles.

My beta readers were equally invaluable, offering thoughtful suggestions and posing questions that made me rethink and refine my work. Their insights helped me understand just how unique my experiences were, often in ways I hadn't realized. What could have been an isolating revelation instead became a deeper connection, thanks to their openness and curiosity. Cindy Thomas, Elizabeth Bohannon, Steve Mullen, Karen Deaver, Laura Hovden, Monique Mayo, Carina Moravec, Kate Schertz, Anne Midler, Eliane Dohemann, Laurie Flynn, and Calla Jacobson—I thank you all. Margaret Evans edited an early version and fixed a lot of my missing or extra commas.

To my husband, Steve Mullen: your steadfast support has meant the world to me. You endured countless dinner-table discussions with infinite patience and requested to read not one but three drafts of this book. What a gift your curiosity and interest in my life's journey has been.

My circle of friends has been a pillar of strength over the years. Cindy

Thomas, my best friend since our college dorm days, has been my rock for over four decades. My college friends, my nursing friends, my work friends, my hiking friends, and my TCK/expat friends—there are too many to name, but you know who you are and I love you for being a part of the emotional fabric that holds me together.

I've had incredible mentors who guided me in the craft and business of writing. Nina Schuyler, who teaches at Stanford University and Book Passage, shared her expertise generously. Lisa Liang, a fellow TCK and creator of *Alien Citizen: An Earth Odyssey*, offered invaluable cross-cultural perspectives. Allison Lane of Allison Lane Literary is a master of marketing. Alison Singh Gee at UCLA Extension provided fresh approaches to travel writing. Don George, travel writer extraordinaire and former editor of the *San Francisco Chronicle* travel section, jumpstarted my travel writing career with his six-week course at Book Passage and has been a valued mentor ever since. My travel writing group—born out of Tim Cahill's workshop at the Travel Writers and Photographers Conference at Book Passage—has been a nourishing source of inspiration.

Finally, my publisher, Linda Stirling, made my heart sing when she told me it would be her honor to publish my book at The Publishing Circle. Her support throughout the editing and publishing process has been a joy to experience, and I love being a part of her team.

USA
San Francisco ★

Peru
Piura ★

West Pakistan
Lahore

East Pakistan
Dacca

Indonesia
Jakarta

1960s Map of the World

Table of Contents

ACKNOWLEDGMENTS x

MAP xii

AUTHOR'S NOTE xvi

1 Voyage to Asia 3

2 Welcome to West Pakistan 11

3 Home Leave/Leave Home 27

4 Culture Clash in California 45

5 Troubled Waters in Peru 65

6 Exploring Peru 81

7 San Francisco City Life 97

8 Soft Landing in East Pakistan 105

9 The Birth of a Country 119

10 Adolescent Angst in Marin 131

11 Freedom in Chico 151

12 Indonesia Bound. 161

13 A New Beginning in Oakland 171

14 Adventures in Asia 177

15 Finding Myself 191

EPILOGUE: Untethered. 207

AFTERWORD. 219

ABOUT THE AUTHOR 224

Author's Note

During the writing of this book, nagging doubts lurked in the back of my mind. For certain events, I wondered if this was my story to tell. What right had I to identify with a place? Not only was I not Pakistani or Peruvian or Indonesian, I was a white girl with a privileged US passport. However, I was deeply affected by what I lived through, side by side with citizens of those countries. The fact is that my life, my story, my identity was forever altered by my experiences in those places. I absorbed a little or a lot of every place I lived, every culture I was exposed to, every house I was invited into, every person who shared a bit of their life with me. I became a product of all those lives.

Decades later, I still feel the intense emotions of the moment. The pleasure of kicking a ball with local Peruvian kids. Gliding my fingers through the lily pads as we drifted through the lake in Kashmir. The taste of sweet mango our Pakistani cook sliced for me. I remember how my body shook with fear when I heard machine guns in the street, and how the acrid smell of burning bodies pricked my nose. These are the memories I can share.

Memories, of course, are fraught with irregularities. If only they were recorded like movies on celluloid so we could replay them and verify shadowy recollections. If writing a memoir was only a retelling of a story, it could be quick and easy. I was so fortunate that when I had the idea for the book, my father was still alive. Even his ever-sharp mind grew fuzzy around the edges in his mid-nineties and we debated which order we lived in places, both of us shocked that it was no longer indelibly recorded in our memory banks.

I spent hours during the pandemic, when my creative juices were turned off, decoding a large stack of passports for our small family of me, Mom, and Dad. Mom had passed away a year earlier, but her memory was notoriously slippery—she was better at remembering a mood, rather than a specific date. A spreadsheet bloomed and became my reference for my life, with every entry, exit and visa noted with country, date and corroborating notes.

I didn't have the benefit of boxes of childhood memorabilia stacked in a garage, like those meticulously saved by parents of friends. Our frequent, sometimes hasty, moves meant there was little in the way of school papers, or report cards, and for some countries, hardly any photos. I found useful information in history books, Time Magazine archives, library archives of master's theses on developing countries, World Bank reports from the projects my father worked on, and photos and recollections from strangers I met on Facebook who lived in the same countries at the same time.

Place names change and so do accepted spellings. For the most part, I've used the names and spellings that existed at the time. East and West Pakistan were the country names when we lived there; they are now called Bangladesh and Pakistan. Dacca is now spelled Dhaka.

Conversations reflect the general mood that matches what I remember and have been reconstructed as truthfully as I could. The chronology is accurate, but some events have been compressed or expanded to aid the narrative flow.

Some people's names have been changed, especially if I don't remember the names or haven't been in touch in decades. There are no composite characters.

I've relayed my story to the best of my ability. I was very young in the beginning of the book so my memory might not have been entirely perfect. Mom and Dad had both passed away by the time the book was finished, the only true fact checkers I could have had.

Between Worlds

An Expat's Quest for Belonging

INGA AKSAMIT

a memoir

the publishing CIRCLE.

1

Voyage to Asia

Lying on the thin mattress, I listen to the rat-a-tat-tat of gunfire, hoping the windowless outside wall in our Dacca, East Pakistan house is thick enough to stave off bullets. Mom and Dad move around restlessly, Dad orbiting the interior perimeter of the house between rounds, Mom's soft reassuring words belying the worry lines drawn across her face.

The fighting feels close, much closer than ever before. I'm thirteen years old and it's my second war. I'll bet there will be a second military evacuation and a second forced separation from Dad in my future. If we can get out, what will I bring in the one small bag I'll be allowed? My favorite doll, Chuz, for sure. Beyond that, it doesn't matter. Things don't matter. All that matters is that we're safe.

When I was four, I had no idea what it would mean to move from California to Pakistan. Now, at the cusp of my teen years, I am no stranger to conflict zones around the world. Our moves always started off with so much promise and potential.

3

* * *

TOKYO

As I stand next to my mother on the Tokyo railway platform, her hand loosely holds mine in a sea of men's legs. The fabric of their dark suits brushes my skin, sticky with sweat in the close air, but I'm determined to hold my position. My short legs, sturdy for a four-year-old, shift as the crowd pushes and pulls. My doll, Chuz, dangles from my hand, her arms and legs akimbo. I'm chafing in the stiff white blouse atop my blue-and-white checkered skirt. Mom, looking nervous, fishes the note from the hotel clerk out of her purse, snaps her purse shut, and shows the note to a man standing next to us. She has her traveling outfit on: a loose orange midi skirt and white top with orange leaves, high heels, and the small handbag on her arm. She provides the only accent of color in this crowd.

The man nods his head vigorously, pointing down the track, repeating "Fuji" over and over. Mom's face relaxes with a smile.

We're in the right spot. Hundreds of eyes are trained on the tracks. Shrill bells announcing the arrival of the train slice through the low murmur of Japanese voices and cigarette smoke in the July heat. The crowd presses closer.

Mom grips my hand tighter as the train glides in. When the doors fly open, I tug on Mom's hand, but she holds me back as a knot of black-haired people streams off the train. The tide shifts as people around us push forward. The gap between the platform and the train widens like a river before my eyes. What looked like a thin black line when I spied it from the back of the crowd is now a yawning gulf. Will my little legs make it?

Mom seems to fly over the gap, her high heels landing on the floor of the train, but my hand slips out of hers. The current keeps surging, and people fill the space between me and Mom. I freeze on the edge of the gap. It seems so big. Mom moves toward me with her hand outstretched, but her fingers are out of reach. A horrifying, dreamlike film plays in my head. In the movie, the doors snap shut, the train pulls away, and I am left standing on the platform. The train carries Mom far, far away and I . . . What happens to me? Will I be left here? Would a Japanese family take me in? Would Mom be able to come back?

All I know is Mom is on one side of the gap and I'm on the other. I clutch my doll to my chest and stop breathing. All I can see is this door and this platform. How will she find me? People are talking all around me, but I can't understand what they are saying. I try to scream, but my throat is so tight no sound comes out. After endless, unmeasurable time, Mom reaches over the gap and yells, "Inga, jump," as she grabs my hand and pulls me onto the train. The doors slide together, breaking the spell, and I dissolve into heaving sobs. All eyes are on me as Mom holds me close, murmuring, "You're safe, honey. You're safe."

But I can't speak. My ears still ring with my silent scream.

* * *

In July 1962, my mother and I were midway through a two-week vacation in Japan.

I was learning that travel wasn't always as much fun as Mom and Dad had promised. This was no ordinary holiday, like visiting Yosemite or Mt. Shasta a couple of hours from our home in Vacaville, California. Tokyo was but one stop on our long journey to join my father in Lahore, West Pakistan. He'd left weeks ago to find us a house and start his new job as Chief Field Engineer with Tipton and Kalmbach Engineers.

When Mom and Dad told me we were moving from Vacaville to West Pakistan, I didn't care. What did I know? It was just another word to learn. Was Pakistan further than San Francisco, where we got our passport photos? The map of the big ocean between here and there meant nothing to me, though I could tell Mom was excited to go, telling everyone we knew that she was finally fulfilling her dream of living overseas. I had only the vaguest idea about Dad's job—something to do with moving water around, like some of the roadside canals in Putah Creek he had pointed out from our car trips.

But now, after our Pan Am flight across the Pacific, jet lag had me alternately up, wide-eyed in the middle of the black night and cranky in the brilliant mid-afternoon sun. And instead of my familiar backyard, I must worry about losing Mom on the train tracks.

Mom bubbled over with excitement about the fancy Imperial Hotel in Tokyo that some man named Frank built, but I did my best to ignore her, annoyed about wearing dress-up clothes all the time, instead of the soft playsuits I wore in Vacaville.

"Do you know how lucky we are to have money from Dad's company to stay here? We'd never be able to afford such a nice place. I'll show you why it's so special. Frank Lloyd Wright likes to use natural materials and colors to blend with the environment. See how he uses sky blue, that reddish color that looks like dirt, and the soft green that looks like moss?"

I didn't understand her comments, but the reddish brick walls in the huge lobby felt warm and cozy. Maybe that's what she meant. I wanted to squish the soft green carpeting with my toes but one look from Mom and the shoes stayed on. I wished I could reach the red tassels dangling from the long white tubular lights splashed with playful red, blue, and yellow dots hanging from the ceiling. While Mom got directions from the concierge, I positioned Chuz, my Madame Alexander doll, in the overstuffed brown leather chairs. I tucked her limp body, clad in a simple white dress, against the back of the chair, smoothed her yellow hair and carefully positioned her firm rubber limbs in place. With her chubby cheeks and blue eyes that closed when she was lying down, she looked different from all the black-haired Japanese people in the lobby. Chuz had been my constant companion since I was born, when she had been bigger than me in my crib. Now, I was much taller, but we still fit side-by-side in the big chairs. Once we were settled, I pointed out all the different colors I could find in the lobby.

At dinner, when Mom reached into her purse to check our tickets and passport, some small photos fell out. I leaned over to pick them up.

"You can look at pictures, but be careful. We might need photos for visas, and you remember what an ordeal it was to find a photographer."

I remembered the long day driving into San Francisco to sit for hours in the small photography studio in one of the tall buildings downtown. I looked at the black-and-white photo of me and Mom sitting close together since we had one passport between us. Mom's dark brown bobbed hair looked black, contrasting with her fair skin and fine features, while my lighter brown hair caught more of a shine from the photographer's bright light. The photo couldn't capture our matching green eyes, and only the top of Mom's collared dress and my striped sailor outfit were visible. We both looked serious, as if to emphasize that this passport was not for fun, but for a big move.

HONG KONG

By the time we got to the Empress Hotel in Hong Kong, on the next leg of our journey, I'd had it with travel and another formal hotel where I had to behave properly, but Mom was nervous, practically giddy between all the latest fashions displayed in the shop windows and it being our last night before who-knows-what she would find in Pakistan. To me, it was one more big hotel lobby, but the voices were much louder than in Japan.

"It's our last night of vacation. You'd better take a nap so we can eat at Gaddi's, that lovely French restaurant downstairs. I'll go make a reservation while you rest. You'll need to be on your best behavior."

I made a face. I hated naps.

Mom turned out the light and tucked me into the huge bed with Chuz. As soon as the door closed, I threw back the covers and took a test jump on the mattress to see how springy it was. By the time she returned with the reservation and a shopping bag, sweat dripped down my face and I panted like a dog on a hot day. Chuz had bounced off the bed in a heap on the floor.

"What's going on in here?"

"Nothing, just napping."

"Bad girl." She looked stern, then softened. "I guess it's all been a bit much for you." She set the shopping bag down and pulled out a pair of stiletto heels with jewel-toned rhinestones.

"Sparkly shoes? Did you get me anything?"

"Sorry, they didn't have anything for kids. Come on, time to get ready for dinner."

I had to take a nap, but Mom got to go shopping? That didn't seem fair. And now I had to get dressed up again?

"Can we eat in the room?" We had done that one night in Japan—no scratchy dress and no sitting still, waiting for our food.

"No, I'm excited to eat here. It's supposed to be one of the best restaurants in Hong Kong and we might not see another nice restaurant for a long time."

No restaurants? Where were we going? To the end of the world? All I knew was that I didn't want one more dinner in one more itchy dress where we had to wait for one more endless meal to be served. How about a hamburger patty with catsup, like home, instead of sukiyaki? Or tuna casserole instead of egg rolls? An hour later, after Mom crammed me into a frilly blue dress trimmed in white lace with black patent leather shoes, we headed down to the formal dining room at Gaddi's French Restaurant, all white tablecloths and forks tinkling against fine china, huge crystal chandeliers, and the savory smell of roast beef filling the room.

I sat in the chair, fidgeting with Chuz, at my limit of being a good girl every minute. Why couldn't I be myself, like in Vacaville? Why wasn't Dad here to help me? He could always reason with Mom. I kicked at the long, white tablecloth, noticing how dark and quiet and inviting it looked behind the fabric. The gold carpet beckoned. While Mom was talking to the server, I slipped off my chair into a cool, shadowy world under the table where I could sit cross-legged with Chuz in my lap and not be stared at.

"What are you doing down there? Come out and sit in your chair this minute. You're going to cause a scene." But I wouldn't come out and eventually Mom realized that if she tried to pull me out, there was definitely going to be a scene.

Under the table, I was safe with Chuz in my luxury tent, enclosed in the folds of rich, white linen that protected me from the rest of the world. The sounds of ice cubes dropping into crystal goblets, the occasional pop of a cork coming out of a wine bottle, and the indistinct murmur of genteel conversation were the backdrop to my now-cozy world. The wait staff tried to coax me out to no avail. They twittered in rapid-fire Chinese, but finally retreated. Mom proceeded with her dinner in relative peace, apparently resigned to the situation.

When the wait staff brought Mom's coffee, they had a surprise. They brought a handful of origami cranes, gently lifted the edge of the tablecloth, and held them toward me. Mom didn't think it would work, but the colorful shapes drew me out. They stroked my hair and pulled the chair out for me. I climbed up in the chair with the colorful cranes and happily ate vanilla ice cream. Mom looked relieved and thanked the staff. Noisy scene averted, child happily eating ice cream for dinner, Mom full of prime rib.

"That wasn't the easiest day, but we got through it. You'll go straight to bed because we have another big day tomorrow. Do you remember what happens tomorrow?" Mom was using her serious voice, but I was glad I wasn't in trouble for hiding under the table.

"Daddy. And Pak-is-tan." I sounded out the name of the country slowly. I didn't want to go to a place called Pakistan; I wanted to go home. But Daddy was in Pakistan. It was a tricky puzzle I couldn't solve. I wanted to get back to our normal life with the three of us together.

Little did I know how different life would be in a big Muslim city in South Asia for a girl from a small town in Northern California.

2

Welcome to West Pakistan

ARRIVAL

As we made our descent to the Lahore International Airport, Mom kept fussing with her hair, outlining her lips with red lipstick, smoothing her dress, and then smoothing mine while I wiggled in my seat, looking out the window to find Dad in the scrum behind the fence.

"We're going to see Daddy in just a bit. Do we have everything? Put your origami bird in the Pan Am bag." She talked a little too fast while checking and double checking our passports and paperwork, excited to see Dad after several months of separation and nervous about confronting Pakistan, a place most of our friends and family had never heard of.

We walked down the steep portable staircase onto the baking tarmac, only to recoil at the stench of garbage from a nearby dump. It wasn't

11

just the garbage, but a complex blend of odors—raw sewage, jet fuel, diesel exhaust, body odor, and curry spices. Mom choked a little and put her hand over her mouth. I pinched my nose and breathed through my mouth.

Everyone looked so different from people we had seen in Japan and Hong Kong. Men were dressed in wool caps and baggy trousers with flowing tunics. Some people were draped in full-length, black robes, covered from head to toe. They were like dark ghouls gliding silently across the polished tile floors in the airport. I stared. Mom stared.

"Mommy, they're wearing pajamas," I said, pointing at the men. "And how can those people see?"

"Try not to point—that's not polite. That's how the men dress. I read about their clothes. That outfit is called *shalwar kameez*, and the caps are made from the soft wool of Karakul sheep. And it's part of their culture for the women to be covered in public. They can see out of that mesh fabric over their eyes. Try not to stare, though. I need to duck into the bathroom. Oh, look there's Daddy."

I caught sight of my father towering over a clot of Pakistani men, his light brown hair contrasting with a sea of black-haired heads. I started to run toward him until Mom grabbed my hand, threw him a wave, and herded me straight into the women's restroom. She parked me outside the stall with strict instructions.

"Do not move."

I stood still, listening to her retching.

"Mommy?" What was wrong with her? I couldn't imagine.

"I'll be fine." She tried to sound bright, but another wave of vomiting overtook her. She emerged, dabbing at her smudged red lips with a tissue before heading to the small mirror above the sink to repair her lipstick. When we finally got through customs, we hurried outside to Daddy, who held out his tanned arms to embrace us both in a big bear hug. He pulled back to get a long look at us, perhaps noticing her pale face contrasting with her bright red lipstick.

"Everything OK?" he asked.

"The smell. The smells got to me, but I'm so happy to see you. We missed you so much." With a wide smile, she flung her arms around his neck while I grabbed onto their legs. When they finally pulled apart, Daddy folded his slim six-foot frame so he could pick me up. I snuggled into his neck, inhaling his familiar All Spice aftershave. Our little family was together again.

Dad had found us a temporary home, a large house with four bedrooms surrounded by a concrete wall topped with pointy pieces of green, brown, and colorless broken glass. I liked how the sun glinted off the different colors like a stained-glass mosaic with sharp edges. Mom looked at the wall.

"Is that necessary? It seems so extreme."

"Lots of houses have it here. There are people who struggle to have enough to eat and a big house like this can be a target for thieves," said Dad in his usual quiet, composed way. "This is just temporary until the Pakistani government finishes building a special compound just for expats working on the WAPDA project." As we walked toward the house, we heard a kind of singing or chanting.

"What is WAPDA again?" asked Mom.

"It stands for the West Pakistan Water and Power Development Authority. It's a mouthful, so we just call it WAPDA," said Dad.

"What's that sound?" I asked.

"It's the Islamic call to prayer from the neighborhood mosque," said Dad.

"What does Isla … Islam … what did you call it?"

"Islam is the religion most Pakistanis follow. You know how Grandma and Grandpa in Texas are Presbyterian? Islam is another religion."

"I like the song. It's different," I said.

"It's nice. It sounds so exotic. Do they do it very often?" asked Mom.

"Five times a day, every day. It doesn't last that long, though," said Dad.

"Wow, that's a lot. There's so much to get used to," she said.

He opened the front door, and I pushed between Mom and Dad to run down the hallway of our new home, only to run smack into a man with dark skin, smooth black hair, and very loose, very white pants and a long white top with a slit up the sides. I looked up in surprise. Who was this?

"Good afternoon, Sahib and Memsahib," the man said to Dad and Mom as he smiled down at me. Other men with big smiles appeared from the back of the house and Dad introduced us to Mohammed, Ahmed, Hassan, Bashir, and Yusuf. I had no idea what this was all about.

"Carroll, you said we might have household help. Why do we need so many?" asked Mom.

"You'll see when we go to the market. You need a driver to take you wherever you go, a cook to gather all the food from different markets— there's the fish market, the meat market, the vegetable market and things like oil and spices come from other markets. You'll need a housekeeper to clean the house and wash the clothes with a wringer washer. There's no dryer—they have to hang the clothes to dry. Wait until you see the iron filled with chunks of red-hot charcoal. And we need a day and night watchman. I checked around with some of the men's wives and they told me this was what most families have. Their wages are so low that they hardly cost anything compared to what we'd pay in the States. We'll pay them a fair salary. You can even get an *ayah*, a nanny, to help take care of Inga."

My head snapped up.

"I don't think so. I'll take care of her. I don't know what to do with all these people and I certainly don't need help with Inga. I majored in Home Economics in college, for heaven's sake. I know how to take care of a house."

Whew, I was glad to hear that. But maybe it would be nice to have someone to play with when Mom and Dad were busy, which was too often.

"Let's just see how it goes. I hired a small group with terrific references who worked for other expat families. They already know how to cook American food and boil water to make it safe for us to drink. That alone takes a lot of time every day. You can add more people if you need more help."

Despite Dad's reassurance to Mom that it was safe, he patrolled the perimeter of the house, testing window latches and door handles to make sure they were secure, and he checked that the night watchman was in his place and awake.

"All set; we're tucked in for the night," he said. This was a ritual that he would repeat every night, despite having a night watchman looking out for us.

The next day, Dad had to go to his job at the offices of Tipton and Kalmbach, a Colorado-based private company doing work for the Pakistan government. As the Chief Field Engineer, he had to visit the job sites where tube wells were being installed to improve drainage, but he was home most nights to hear about Mom's travails with the help.

It sounded so luxurious to have servants, as if we were suddenly rich and famous, but we were neither. It didn't take long for the shine to rub off for Mom. The first crew was not a good match.

"They won't listen to me. I don't want them around," said Mom the moment he opened the front door one day in the second week.

"They did what I told them before you got here."

"That's because you hired them, and they think of you as their boss. All I get are sweet smiles and gentle 'Yes, memsahibs' before they disappear."

"It will get easier, I promise."

It didn't, and soon Mom was agitating to let them go.

"Let's go to the market then. You can see what it's like and decide if you need them or not."

I was excited to see this market and get out of the house. We piled into the car with the driver and wound through narrow streets, making jerky progress to avoid hitting any people, cows, mangy dogs, or small children scrabbling in the dirt, many clad only in a dirty t-shirt, sometimes with no pants. Every person we passed had thick, shiny, black hair that gleamed with oil. When we got out of the car, people stared, crowded closely around us, and reached out to touch my arms or my hair.

Dad towered over the much shorter Pakistani men. Even Mom, at five feet four inches, was taller than most.

"They aren't used to seeing light colored hair," Dad said, flicking his hands to wave the crowd away, unperturbed. I was relieved when they retreated a couple of feet, but they followed closely behind as we walked through the market. We slowly gathered a bigger crowd the longer we were there. Looking at the ground, I hoped to avoid attracting more attention. I didn't like being touched. Looking up briefly, I searched for a building that looked like a grocery store.

"Where's the market?" I asked.

"This is the market. It's all open air, not like the supermarket back home." Each stall was covered with a roof of fabric or corrugated metal, and some were only a couple of feet wide. We had to watch every step to avoid sliding through dog poop, rotting mango, or an open sewer.

"Dorothy, you'll have to learn to bargain if you're going to shop here. I'll start us off," said Dad, haggling with the shopkeepers as if it was his last rupee at stalls piled high with colorful vegetables and fruit. Women dressed in multicolored saris, long tunics with loose pants, or in full *purdah*, bargained fiercely next to us. There were different sections for fresh fish mounded on top of ice, whole plucked chickens lying naked with heads and feet still attached, and huge meat carcasses—covered with flies as the heat rose—that hung on giant hooks. I plugged my nose. When I took some test puffs of air, I nearly gagged, but eventually I learned to walk through the market breathing normally.

After a few rounds of bargaining, Mom purchased several pounds of cucumbers and onions and later filled the kitchen with clattering pots and the strong, acrid scent of vinegar as she tried her hand at canning Grandma's sweet bread-and-butter pickle recipe. I tried to help, but every time I stirred the big bowl of sliced cucumbers, they spilled out of the bowl and made a mess. Mom let me shake the salt over the cucumbers to draw the moisture out. Then I got to use the measuring spoons to add the right amount of white sugar and yellow turmeric into the bubbling pot of vinegar. The pickles were perfect: sweet, full of tangy, bright flavor, and they had a satisfying crunch.

"It feels good to make something familiar, but I see what you mean about needing help. I'm exhausted after one trip to the market. It would take me all day to gather the ingredients for one meal, much less for all the canning and baking I want to do," said Mom.

"I'm going to love pickles on my roast beef sandwiches with your bread. You can decide later about who you want to keep," said Dad.

After a rocky start, we gradually adjusted to Lahore life. Mom, unique among her friends, got a driver's license and drove herself to the market occasionally. She learned to haggle. And after shedding many tears of frustration, she found the confidence to fire the entire crew of people Dad had hired. She asked new expat friends for recommendations and hired a smaller team who were loyal to her, not Dad. She was happier after that and appreciated the help.

SCHOOL

"Mrs. Anderson invited us to tea today. Maybe she'll become a good friend. It will be good for me to have friends here. You'll be on your best behavior, won't you?" Mom, dressed in her slim pencil skirt and high heels, laid out a frilly dress, lacy white socks, and black patent leather shoes for me.

Mrs. Anderson welcomed us into her front room and called for her servant to bring tea. When he left the room, she said, "It's such a hard place to live, isn't it? How are you settling in?"

I ran through my mental list of things that were different. Some were pleasant, like the drawn-out melodic rhythm of the call to prayer. Some were disturbing, such as the crippled children begging in the street and the bloody animal carcasses hanging in the open-air markets. Some were annoying, such as the flies.

"There's plenty to figure out, but it's not a bad place," said Mom.

"But what about the SERvants," said Mrs. Anderson, drawing out the first part of the word.

The servants? What about them, I wondered. Once Mom had the

ones she wanted, they did so much for us. We were so lucky to have people who brought food to the house, cooked it for us, and washed our clothes. They gave me fresh mango and made sure I had snacks.

"It's not so bad. I love it here," said Mom. A moment of stillness grew into an uncomfortable pause, which blossomed into an unbearable silence broken only by the sound of Mrs. Anderson slowly stirring sugar into her cup. What was going on? The room was suddenly tense, but I didn't know what happened. My dress itched, and I stared at my patent leather shoes. I turned my head to ask Mom a question, but a firm hand on my knee and sideways glance put a stop to that.

Mrs. Anderson tried again. "Well, you have to keep a sharp eye on them or they'll steal you blind."

"I haven't had any problems."

"You must miss home, at least? Where did you grow up?"

"No, I don't. I hated growing up in Texas. I spent my entire childhood plotting how I was going to get out. That's why I became a flight attendant for TWA after college. I'm thrilled I found a husband who wants to travel and couldn't be happier that we're here.

"He worked in Afghanistan for four years before he met me and shared so many wonderful stories. I feel very lucky that we landed here with this job assignment, so we can experience some of what he's already had."

"Is your husband with the State Department?"

"No, he's the Chief Irrigation Engineer for Tipton and Kalmbach. They're working on a project with the West Pakistan Water and Power Development Authority. It's so interesting—they are working on ways to reduce salinity and improve agriculture in the Indus Valley."

Bored, I played with Chuz while Mrs. Anderson fiddled with teacups, murmuring, "Fascinating, I'm sure."

We left as soon as the tea was drunk, just as Mrs. Anderson was explaining all the benefits of joining the American Women's Club of Lahore. "I'll think about it," said Mom.

In the back seat of the car, Mom grumbled all the way home. "Can you believe it? It's just what I was afraid of. All these small-minded American women who just want to complain and compare everything to home. Even the servants! We're so fortunate to have the help. I mean, I had my issues with the first crew, but that's only because they were loyal to Dad. The ones we have now are great. We're never going to be like that. Okay?"

"Okay," I said, not knowing what else was expected of me.

"Forget the American Women's Club. I can't imagine being around a bunch of people like that."

A few weeks later, we were at another tea, but things were going better with Mrs. Jones, a woman that Mom liked because she didn't complain all the time.

"You should go down to the new American school and get Inga enrolled," said Mrs. Jones. "Chet loves it. He's in first grade and has met so many friends."

Chet was my best, and currently only friend, even though he was a grade ahead of me. That's why I didn't have anyone to play with today— because he was in school. I kept quiet. *School? Could I really be a Big Girl already?*

"That'll be the first thing I do when she's old enough to go to school. Believe me, I'm ready," said Mom. What did she mean by ready? Was she thinking about the time I didn't clean my room and talked back? I had hoped that if I put it off long enough, the maid would do it, but Mom insisted that I do some chores, just like I would if we were in the States. She chased me down the hallway after that, waving the bright green flyswatter with the pink plastic flower. When she flicked the back of my legs, all the pink petals fell off and she fell down laughing in spite of her frown. I laughed, too, but eyed the flyswatter warily. The swats didn't hurt that much, but I wished I could run fast enough to escape them.

"How old is she? She looks like she's five."

"She's only four, just tall for her age."

"Oh, I doubt that they'd care. The school just opened a few years ago, so they're begging for students. They're expecting the expat community to grow, but so far, they aren't anywhere near full. Besides, it's best to start early because most of these expat kids end up losing a year with all the travel. That's important if you're planning on living overseas long term. You'll be doing her a favor to start her early. That way, by the time she hits high school, she'll be the right age."

"I never thought of that."

When we were back in the car, I said, "Mommy, am I really going to go to school?"

"We'll go down there and see. Would you like that?"

"I guess. How would I lose a year?"

"Losing a year is when kids get held back and have to repeat a grade if they can't keep up. Don't worry. That won't happen to you." Mom swerved to avoid a cow. "But maybe you should start early, just in case."

That was all it took. Mom hatched a new plan for getting me out from underfoot. Off we went to get me registered at the Lahore American School where they accepted me into the morning kindergarten class. The school was a two-story, white-washed concrete building with a curved front portico and wide, outdoor staircases at the ends of the building that led to the school yard out back.

I wasn't sure what the other kids would look like, but when Mom dropped me off at my classroom on the first day, most of the little kids looked like classmates I might have had in Vacaville—girls with blonde or brown hair, most dressed in suspender skirts; boys in dark pants and white shirts. There were a few Pakistani kids wearing *shalwar kameez*. After meeting at least eight Pakistani children with the Khan surname, including a boy named Ayub Khan, the same name as the President of Pakistan, I figured it was a common name or they were all in the same family.

I loved school. I immediately abandoned the reserved air that I adopted around adults and ran around talking to all the other kids. Sitting still was hard in my overstimulated state.

"Inga, is there something you'd like to share with the class?" the teacher would say nearly every day, staring down at me as she stood next to my chair, interrupting my conversation. I reluctantly learned to sit quietly in a group, practice my letters, and lie down for a nap—never willingly.

I practiced the alphabet on special paper with dotted lines to keep the different parts of the letters from drifting off the page. Lessons were in English, but we also learned some Urdu, the language of Pakistan. I learned to count from one to ten in both English and Urdu. "Ek, do, teen, chaar, paanch, che, saat, aath, nau, dus," I'd chant at home in a sing-song voice.

I made so many friends and learned how to play jacks and tic-tac-toe. School was so much better than I expected. Until report cards came out.

What were report cards? No one had explained those to me. When she picked me up in our car, Mom frowned when she read aloud the teacher's comments on my first report card.

"Inga is bright but prefers to socialize with other children," was the first of a long string of report card comments that echoed the theme of my precocious self who would rather maintain a running commentary with kids sitting next to me than focus on lessons. "You'd better show this to Dad when he gets home."

I held the card behind my back as I walked into the living room when Dad returned from work.

"What do you have in your hands?" Dad asked.

"Nothing."

"Let me see." This went back and forth a few times until I handed it over. He examined it carefully.

"It sounds like you're playing with your friends when you should be learning to read and write. Is that true?"

"I don't know ... " I trailed off.

"An Aksamit must always try hard. You need to do better," Dad said in his stern voice.

"I'll try," I said, my face hot with shame. I wanted to work hard to please Daddy. Mom always used more words than Dad, so his few words carried more importance. I wasn't too happy that the teacher tattled on me. I hadn't understood how the reporting system worked, and that was a big betrayal.

We settled into our routines. Dad went to work, Mom went to the market, and I went to school just like any other traditional American family in the stereotype of the times.

The new expat compound we moved to was full of single-family and multi-unit homes encircled by a concrete wall. Most of the families had kids, so it was easy to find playmates. My friend from school, Lisa, was my best friend on hot days because she had a pool in her backyard. I coveted that pool and would have gone over every day, but Mom said we had to wait for an invitation.

Chet, with his swagger and blond buzz cut, lorded over me with how smart he was because he was a year ahead in school. He liked to boss me around and laughed at how I didn't know how to play any games. I didn't care—his toy collection was impressive, and he was my best friend when I wanted to play rough and tumble games. He was a fast runner and always found good places to hide when we played hide-and-seek. I had never heard of croquet, but he taught me how to knock the colorful wooden balls through hoops using a mallet from an old beat up set they inherited from a family leaving Lahore. I was glad there was no report card for play time.

* * *

"Inga, don't bother the servants. They don't need you underfoot."

If Mom couldn't find me in the house, she knew I would be hanging around out back. Unlike my mother, I enjoyed having the servants around. They were always nice to me and gave me slices of mango or papaya. When they were working, I sat on the string *charpoy* bed used by the servants to relax on the back porch during their frequent breaks. Five times a day, they stopped what they were doing to pray, coinciding with the times we heard the *muezzin's* call to prayer, usually followed by an extended break.

I was fascinated by the *dhobie-wallah*, who handled our laundry. He gracefully swept the heavy, metal iron filled with red-hot charcoal back and forth to smooth the wrinkles in my father's shirts, placing another cloth over the shirt to catch any bits of black charcoal that fell out of the iron. The *chowkidar,* our watchman, just seemed to sit around, but I supposed that was okay, as long as he wasn't asleep.

During the long hours when I was at home with Mom, I had new playmates: Little Boy and Little Girl. I don't know why my imaginary friends didn't have more interesting names; that's what they called themselves. They helped me choose colored crayons for my coloring book, read my comic books with me, dressed Chuz in different outfits that Mom made when her Singer electric sewing machine arrived in the shipment from the States, and had tea with me using my tea set. I told them about my day at school and they listened patiently.

* * *

Mom picked me up one day after I had been playing with Lisa and Chet at his house. I couldn't wait to tell her what I had seen. "Guess what I saw? You have to guess. Never mind, you'll never guess. Trolls. They both had trolls."

"What are trolls? I've never heard of them outside of a fairytale."

"They're dolls, but they look funny, with thick arms and legs and crazy hair that sticks out all over. Lisa's had bright pink hair and Chet's had lime green hair. You'll have to see them. Can I get one?"

"I don't even know what they are, and I don't know if you can have one. They probably don't have them for sale here."

"But I neeeeeeed one." I pouted, sticking my lower lip out.

A few months later, a colleague of Dad's was visiting the job site from the home office in the States. I met him while the adults were having drinks in the living room before dinner. When he handed me a small package, I looked at Mom, surprised.

"Go ahead. You can open it." I ripped open the package and found a troll—a beautiful troll with pink hair and arms that stuck straight out from his body. I was awestruck. "But how? How did you know? I thought there weren't any here."

"Your Dad wrote me a letter before I left, and I found one in a toy store in Colorado. It wasn't easy to find."

"Thank you. I love it," I exclaimed, holding the troll tightly against my chest. My brain felt like it was going to explode. I had no idea one could send letters to summon special creatures. A delayed summons, but a miracle, nonetheless. Mom was pleased to get some packages, too, and she hurried away with them, murmuring something about Christmas presents. So that's how that worked, I told myself. If you couldn't get something you wanted in Lahore, you had to find someone coming over from the States. Good to know.

We learned about the major holidays in Pakistan such as Pakistan Day, Ramadan, and Eid-al-fatr. Ramadan, a religious holiday when Muslims fast all day for thirty days to honor the revealing of the Koran to Prophet Mohammed. Celebrating the holidays was tough for the workers because they had even less energy than usual, but Mom was understanding and let them alone to rest when they needed to. Eid marks the end of Ramadan when Muslims feast for three days. There were festive celebrations at the school for the major American holidays, including Thanksgiving and Christmas, when Mom would try to get a friend to take her to the state department commissary to get a frozen turkey.

The adults had a constant circuit of expat cocktail parties and dinner dances where I'd usually end up asleep on a pile of coats, and Santa always arrived on a camel, wearing his red suit.

Mom and Dad, both tall and lean, wore their clothes well. Dad, standing tall in his suit, with his strong jawline and quiet demeanor, was dashing, while Mom preened in the latest fashions based on any magazines she could find and replicate on her sewing machine. Mom came alive at parties, swishing her skirt in her high heels, circulating among the guests to talk to everyone with a constant stream of entertaining stories, while Dad usually settled into a chair next to some of his work buddies and talked engineering talk or shared news of the world gleaned from weeks-old copies of *Time Magazine* while sipping on a gin and tonic. He would dance with Mom a little, but if not, there were plenty of men who would twirl her around the floor.

One of my favorite activities before a party was the trip to the icehouse, where gigantic machinery clanked loudly, moving enormous blocks of ice onto beds of straw. Sights that were so strange when we first arrived became normal and we became used to all the different styles of dress and women with varying degrees of purdah.

The crush of traffic in the streets jammed with bicycles, trucks, buses, and cows seemed ordinary now, though I never got used to seeing so many mutilated beggars. Mom told me that bad people sometimes hurt kids on purpose so they'd be blind or disfigured and make more money because people would feel sorry for them. I averted my eyes, imagining the terrible cruelty. We passed long blocks of shanty towns on the outskirts of Lahore, and I wondered how the ones with cardboard roofs held up in the monsoon. I could see that even in the shantytown, there were better quality shanties with corrugated metal roofs and pieces of metal on the sides, but all had dirt floors. The small children were grubby, and their clothes were threadbare and dirty as they kicked a deflated ball around. How could they go to school or study in such small spaces? At least these kids weren't mutilated—they still had their eyes and arms and legs. Even so, it made me sad.

POX

Mom came to my room late one night, wakened by my moaning, finding me sweaty. She put her cool hand on my forehead.

"Wow, you're hot. You have a fever," she said. She ran some cold water on a washcloth, wiped my face with it, folded it, and laid it across my forehead. Dad appeared with the glass thermometer.

"Hold it under your tongue and don't bite it," he said, smoothing my rumpled top sheet. "One hundred and three. That's high. Too high," he said when he read the numbers. Mom stayed with me until I got sleepy. Nightmares woke me from my fevered sleep, especially the one where the train doors slammed shut with me on the track and Mom inside, just like in Japan. I was so relieved to open my eyes and find her sitting beside my bed.

I stayed home from school and then the spots appeared on my chest and back, eruptions that concerned Mom and Dad. Dad looked up my symptoms in his medical book. "It could be smallpox," he announced in his serious voice.

"But we're all vaccinated. How could it be smallpox?" Mom looked scared. She was always easier to read than Dad.

"Vaccinations aren't 100% effective, so it's still possible to get it. Let's hope not, but it's a possibility."

Mom and Dad hovered over me for several days. Mom sponged me off with cool water and tried to keep me from scratching at the itchy sores by playing games, coloring with me, and reading to me. Dad went to work and asked some colleagues about whether there was an English-speaking doctor. A German doctor came to the house and prescribed high doses of antibiotics. Dad came home early every day, rushing to my room to examine the spread of the pox on my back and then my arms and legs. He'd give Mom a break and tell me stories about growing up on the farm in Kansas with his eight siblings and his favorite horse, Pony Boy. Mom kicked the cook out of the kitchen for a time and made me chicken soup. One or the other of them would check on me several times at night, touching my forehead to see if I was feverish.

A few days later, Mom heard from one of the other mothers in the neighborhood that a few other kids had come down with chickenpox at school. Dad compared the two diseases in his book and decided that it was possible it was chickenpox instead of smallpox. Their relief was obvious. I would live another day.

3

Home Leave / Leave Home

D ad got vacation time every year, but every two years, like most expats, we got a free trip from the company to return home for a month. Dad had saved some vacation time, so we had nearly two months for a grand, round-the-world trip for home leave. Home now meant Lahore to me, but Mom explained we'd be going home to America. I barely remembered our California home, so I was excited until I learned we wouldn't be visiting Vacaville.

What did home mean if not Vacaville? Home meant something else to Mom and Dad.

When I asked Mom where we were going, it turned out that we were going to Texas and Kansas to visit both sets of grandparents and I'd see where they lived for the first time. It was strange to think about Mom being a little girl in Texas and Dad being a little boy in Kansas. And it was confusing that home leave meant going home to them, but to me it meant leaving home.

Mom was learning how to stretch the company stipend by

choosing more modest hotels than the ones we used in Japan through recommendations from friends in Lahore. I liked the more relaxed, smaller hotels. The maids and clerks made a fuss over me, and I could wear comfortable clothes.

Each time we stepped off the plane in another country, I felt as though I was starring in a different movie, just like Shirley Temple. In Vienna, towering ornate buildings with spires pointing into the sky made me feel very small. I pictured myself on the big screen swinging onto the streetcars that reminded me of Hong Kong, but without the din of the Chinese crowds. In Copenhagen, I gazed longingly at the Little Mermaid, the bronze statue perched on a rock in the harbor along the Langelinie promenade. I begged Dad to take me back there several times, and he surprised me with a ceramic replica of the graceful girl-serpent that I treasured. When I swam in the heated hotel pool, I tried to capture her mesmerizing pose but lacked her pretty flippers. At Tivoli Gardens, I experienced my first thrilling roller-coaster ride once the terror receded. I marveled at how clean and well-ordered everything was with no honking horns, putrid smells, or cows in the street. Best of all, people didn't stare at me or try to touch my hair. Even though my brown hair differed from all the blonde heads, I blended into the crowd. And the water—it tasted so good. I guzzled it right from the tap, unlike at home, where I had to remember to drink from the pitcher of boiled water. Everything about Europe felt so different from Lahore.

One day we traveled outside of Copenhagen to stay in a small inn surrounded by a peaceful garden and a white picket fence. After dinner, Mom tucked me in early, saying there might be a surprise later. In the middle of the night, she woke me.

"Inga, wake up. There's something you need to see."

"What's wrong?"

"Nothing's wrong. Put your shoes on." She grabbed one foot and slipped one shoe on, then the other. "Come on, follow me." I rubbed my eyes and yawned, wondering what all the fuss was about. "Come on," she said impatiently.

"Outside?" Confused, I trudged sleepily onto the balcony. I could see dark forms of other people standing on the grass. They had their heads tilted back, looking at something.

"Look up," said Mom, pointing to the dark sky. A strange cloud shimmered and undulated in the sky. Vibrant shades of green and red changed shapes, moving higher, then lower, curling back on itself, fading away and then coming back stronger than ever.

"What is it? How did they get those lights up in the sky?"

"It's the Northern Lights. We're so lucky to see them. Special particles from the sun hit gasses in the sky to make the colors, but only at the North and South Poles. It's a special thing up here in Denmark, but it doesn't happen every night."

We went to the lawn and lay down on the soft grass, staring at that amazing light show until it played itself out and faded away.

We exchanged the quiet countryside of Denmark for the bustle and impossibly high skyscrapers of New York City where I felt every sense light up with excitement—the scorching hot pizza that melted the roof of my mouth, the endless line of Yellow Cabs honking even though they couldn't move, the steaming vents from mysterious tunnels under the city, and my uncle, who looked scary in his official pilot's uniform, even though he was the sweetest man ever.

My head was spinning by the time we left New York and flew to Amarillo, a quiet town in the panhandle of Texas, where my maternal grandparents met us. Grandad Deaver wore a suit and Grandma wore a belted dress and pumps with low heels. They took us to a cafeteria for lunch where I eagerly pointed at the food I wanted—so many choices—and a server mounded it onto a plate that became so heavy I could barely lift it. I couldn't eat it all, but I was like a food explorer, loving all the different tastes of barbeque, lasagna, fried chicken, mashed potatoes, French fries, and salad. That salad was for Mom. Who needed salad with so many fun foods?

The two-hour drive from Amarillo to Memphis (the one in Texas, not Tennessee), was monotonous and made me antsy. Memphis turned out to be a speck of a town on high plains dotted with tumbleweeds and cotton fields. Empty red brick streets without people, cows, or wooden carts looked so different from the busy plain asphalt or dirt roads of Pakistan. Cars were parked neatly in driveways, and I could hear a tractor in the distance when we pulled in front of my grandparent's brick house.

The best part about Memphis was meeting Bonita Ballew, a girl my age who lived across the street from my grandparents' house. She pulled her light brown hair from her face with a wide headband—much more elegant than my center part with bangs. She became my trusted guide, taking me all over town to show me off to a tight-knit group of local children. In a town where visitors were a rarity, let alone someone from distant Pakistan, our arrival sparked curiosity, camaraderie, and a newspaper article.

After a few hectic days, we ventured across the skinny panhandle of Oklahoma to Kansas in Grandad's spacious Oldsmobile to visit my paternal grandparents and a parade of cousins I didn't know I had. Dad's parents still carried the spirit of farming, even though they now lived in town in a house with a big vegetable garden and lots of flowers that connected them to the land. Grandma Aksamit wore a loose cotton flower print dress and Grandpa wore dungarees with a plaid shirt. Dad proudly showed me the special set of white china with delicate hand-painted blue flowers he had given his parents. They were so pretty. When I learned he had picked out the set in Copenhagen on his way home from his first overseas post in Afghanistan before he met Mom, I realized what an important place they held in his heart. It was hard for me to imagine that Dad had a life before me, but here was a tangible piece of his journey, with the people he grew up with. That was a lot to think about. After much eating, drinking, socializing, we finally boarded another flight, this time to Hawaii, where I got to swim in the warm ocean, then onto Japan.

Only two years before, Mom and I had been in Japan, but this time it was different. For one thing, Dad was with us. For another, Mom had learned a lot about how to navigate in different countries. Instead of staying in cities, Mom and Dad planned the trip to include seaside stops, traditional *ryokan* inns, and many *onsen* hot springs. We were all relaxed and happy on our magical adventure. After a couple of days in Bangkok, Thailand, a blur of a big Asian city, we headed back to Lahore just in time for me to start second grade.

As soon as we returned home to Lahore, I ran to find the servants. They all had big smiles and Yusuf brought me a dish of sliced mango. I dragged Chuz to my familiar bedroom so we could visit with the troll doll sitting on my narrow bed. I read her some of my *Archie* comics.

When Chet and Lisa knocked at the front door to ask if I could play croquet in the front yard, I yelled "yippee" and ran outside. I thought about how happy Dad had been to see his friends in Kansas. When he had walked into the shops, he had lit up when the shopkeepers shouted his name and slapped him on the back. In Texas, it seemed like everyone in town knew Mom, whether she was in a store or walking down the street. It was so odd—to me it was just another stop, another bed to sleep in, another set of new sights to see. But to them, it was home, the way Lahore was to me.

GRANDMA

One day, as I worked on my spelling in my room, Dad came home a little early. He and Mom went into their bedroom straightaway, and I could hear their low murmur of voices, Dad's a low baritone and Mom's an octave higher, but I couldn't make out the words. Dad didn't say a word at dinner. After ice cream, we went into the living room, and they said they had something to tell me. *Was I in trouble?* I sat down.

"Dad got a telegram today," Mom said. I looked at Dad, but he didn't say anything. "It had some bad news. Your grandmother, your dad's mother, died last week." I had never known anyone to die before.

"Oh, no. That's so sad." Now I understood why there was all the serious adult talk. "But I just got to know her in Kansas. Are you sad?" I asked Dad. I got up and snuggled next to him. He put his arm around my shoulders, and I gave him a hug.

"Yes, of course I'm sad. But I'm OK. I haven't seen her much since I left home to join the Navy during World War II and then went to college. I'll miss her letters. She always filled me in on the news about the family."

"Are we going back to the States?"

"No, I'm afraid we can't. We were just there for home leave, and we wouldn't be able to make it back in time for the funeral," Mom said. This left me feeling out of sorts. It just seemed wrong not to rush off to the airport to do ... what? I didn't know what. I didn't cry, but I felt like I should have.

Dad was usually quiet, especially compared to Mom, who was always talking, but he was even more subdued for a week after he got the news of his mother's death. He'd sit in his chair after work and read, and now and then I'd hear a deep sigh. Mom told me to give him some time without bothering him because he was unhappy about losing his mother.

KASHMIR

One oppressively hot summer, Dad, and some of the engineers he worked with had vacation time coming. They didn't have enough time to go back to the States, so they decided to explore more of Pakistan together. I was thrilled because that meant Chet, who was still my best friend, could come, too, although Mom said to leave the croquet set behind since we'd be on a boat. The servants bustled around the house packing food and clothing for a week-long excursion to Kashmir, 280-miles away in a long-disputed region high in the foothills of the Himalaya. We flew there with three other families.

Departing from Lahore, we skirted the Wagah border with India, an artificial divide that cleaved through the heart of the ancient Punjab region, a place that had shared language, food, traditions, and five major rivers since at least the 16th century. In 1947, as the British prepared to pull out of India, they had a knotty political and religious problem to solve. India wanted to regain their independence and the British rulers agreed, but different political leaders in India wanted different things. A Muslim faction wanted their own region, while other Indian leaders wanted to retain a united India.

The British came up with an audacious solution, known as Partition.

Layers of negotiation and waves of violence resulted in the bloody birth of a new nation, Pakistan, that split two geographic regions, Punjab and Bengal, in half. Part of Punjab went to West Pakistan while part of Bengal went to East Pakistan, an awkward division of 1,000 miles separating the twin bodies of an infant country. The rest of Punjab and Bengal stayed in India. Muslims were allocated the land in Pakistan, while Hindus and Sikhs moved to secular India. Just north of the Punjab region was Kashmir, an area so strategic and beautiful that everyone wanted a piece of it. Kashmir was allowed to decide whether to go with India or Pakistan, but the decision was never fully settled. Even China nibbled away at Kashmir's borders.

I had heard the adults talking about Partition, but I knew none of this as we flew from Lahore, the capital of Punjab, to this special place. I would soon learn more about Partition and the fallout that would affect us.

After we landed, two taxis transported us to Dal Lake. The carved wooden houseboats were magical against the backdrop of the snow-covered Zabarwan Range that flirted with the heavens.

"How charming. I was expecting the houseboats to be rustic, but the intricate carvings and massive timbers make them so ornate," said Mom while Dad directed the houseboy to set our bags down on the houseboat he had reserved.

"Some people say they were built for the British during the Raj, before Partition, because they weren't allowed to own land. Owning boats was a loophole. But others say houseboats have existed in Dal Lake for centuries. I'm not sure what's true or if the houseboats became fancier when the Brits got involved," said Dad.

Frilly curtains gently swayed in the breeze against delicately carved lattice woodwork. Along the gunwales, wide planks allowed passage to the other end. Sofas covered in sky blue silk contrasted with the golden carpeting with red and blue geometric shapes that felt smooth against my bare feet. Light streamed in through the windows, but the dark carved wood paneling made it feel like we were in a mysterious cavern. Chet and I climbed the steep staircase down to the water from the back of our boat. A boatman waved from a long, narrow, wooden *shikara* gondola with pointy ends and a simple canopy to protect passengers from the sun. Mom, standing on the back deck, said we could go with him. We slipped through glassy blue waters dotted with floating white lotus flowers; the large, round, green leaves beckoning like steppingstones for fairies. Boats glided near us, groaning under the weight of cut firewood. Men plucked greens from floating crops near the shore, while women slapped wet clothes on stone steps at the water's edge. Further back, two-, three- and four-story buildings adorned with wooden balconies beckoned.

Back at our houseboat, Chet and I sat cross-legged on the floor with a low cedar coffee table between us while his father taught us how to play checkers. I won my first game, but after that Chet beat me every time until dinner interrupted us. The beef kebabs and rice pilau were delicious, but the lamb flavor was too strong for me, and I wasn't sure about the crunchy fried lotus root. The adults practically swooned over the food; they thought it was so good.

"Why don't we eat like this at home?" Mom said.

"We could. Most cooks hired by expats were trained by the Brits, so that's what they make," said Dad.

"That was nice when we were new. I don't think I was ready to eat Pakistani food every day when we arrived. But now, I'm curious. This is so tasty. I'm going to ask the cook to start making us a few local dishes. It's time we learned more about where we're living. What do you think, Inga?"

"I like most of it. Not all of it. But if there's rice, and it's not too spicy, I'd like it."

When we returned, Mom picked up the 1964 version of *Cooking in Lahore*, produced by the American Women's Club. "This is the only thing they've done that's useful. There are some great recipes here. The first half has Pakistani recipes, and the second has American recipes to teach cooks how to make food for foreigners. At least I know the names of some dishes to ask for. I'm sure they have their own recipes for Pakistani food."

After that, a few times a week at home, we ate mild yellow curry in a thin sauce, beef kebabs grilled over a small charcoal hibachi, mild rice *biryani*, which I liked, *chapati* bread, which Dad loved, always with *dal* soup made with lentils. As soon as the onions and aromatic spices hit the hot oil, they tickled my nose, and I knew we'd be tasting something delicious that night. That made Mom happy, and I liked almost everything.

From Dal Lake, we drove to Gulmarg, a hill station higher in the Himalaya where horse-back riding was a big attraction. The valley was ringed with snow-covered peaks, and pine trees marched down the slopes like toy soldiers in formation. The pint-sized ponies were perfect for my size. Dad lifted me into the saddle. I gripped each side with my pink-panted legs, then grinned at my father. "Now I can ride a horse, too, just like you did with Pony Boy on your farm in Kansas."

The horse-*wallah*, dressed in a loose, long white shirt, dark vest, and Karakul wool cap, placed my feet in short stirrups. I'm sure Mom and Dad expected us to take a sedate walk. The horse-*wallah* had a different plan. I laughed excitedly, urging my horse to go faster, and he obliged with a switch to my horse's behind. Off we went on a wild ride with the horse-*wallah* chasing the horse with the whip and Mom chasing after him with a stick screaming at him to stop. Dad, caught off guard, trailed along behind. Mom's saffron *shalwar* trousers flashed in the bright sun as she ran. She shot angry lasers through her cat-eye sunglasses at both Dad and the horse-*wallah*. I clung to the horse as best I could, my feet in the shortened stirrups, hands white-knuckled on the horn of the saddle as I squealed in delight. I survived. The horse-*wallah's* tip was less than generous. Dad dialed the drama down a notch or two for our next excursion with a quiet trip to Shalimar Gardens along sedate strolling paths.

One afternoon, I lazily held a fishing pole in my hands, content to hang out with Chet and his father on the deck of the houseboat. The sun felt warm on my bare arms, and I watched the blue flash of brightly colored kingfishers swooping over the water. Suddenly, I felt a sharp tug on my line, the tip of the uneven wooden stick dipping toward the water. I jumped up, not knowing what to do, the pole almost sliding from my hands. A servant ran over to hold the pole with me, pulling it this way and that. He had the net ready, slipping it under the glittering fish as it came out of the water. A big, fat golden carp slid into the net. "Dad, hurry, come and see my fish!" I yelled.

He came running with a broad smile on his face. I beamed with delight. But as I watched the vibrant fish steadily lose its vitality, its bright colors vanishing into shades of gray, my heart broke. And when it lay lifeless on the deck, I felt like I took something that didn't belong to me, even though Dad looked so proud. It was a letdown after such a magical moment.

WAR

In September 1965, I labored over the sewing machine in the guest room at the house of one of Dad's coworkers. The tempting sounds of the other kids squealing as they chased a ball outside on the grass distracted me. Sunlight streamed into the room through large panes of glass, the humid air settling heavily around us. I asked Mom, "Can I go play with the other kids?"

"It sounds like the bombing has stopped. Just stick with your sewing a little longer and then you can go outside."

The India-Pakistan War of 1965 had started on August 5 and school had been suspended, but Mom insisted I do some homework or learn something new every day. We had been staying in this large home with other families for several weeks in September, when the fighting near Lahore escalated. Mom had set up her Singer sewing machine on a table on the desk and was teaching me how to sew a dress. We pinned the papery thin Vogue pattern to the fabric and carefully cut out the pieces. The sketch on the front of the pattern showed a close-fitting bodice attached to a full skirt worn by cherubic-looking girls who looked nothing like me, a tomboy.

I concentrated while I cut, the heavy, metal scissors too big for my hand, while mom held the fabric taut over the desk. All was quiet in the house, the other kids having swept through the patio shaded by the giant mango tree on their way out to the lush lawn and garden path. I wondered what I was missing as I bent over my work. Were they playing croquet or hide-and-seek? We laid the cut pieces on the bed and Mom showed me how they were going to fit together. She helped me with the sewing. I sat on the edge of the chair so I could push the pedal with my foot while she guided the fabric. I liked the satisfying feeling of the fabric advancing with a neat line of stitches as we sewed the pieces of the bodice together.

The sound of the kids playing had faded away, but now they ran toward the house, their high-pitched voices piercing the heavy air in the room. My head jerked up. I looked imploringly at Mom.

"OK, that's enough for one day. Go ahead and we'll do some more tomorrow. Don't go wild."

I ran outside just as the gang finished another lap and I raced after them, glad for the company. I ran across the expanse of green grass and met up with them at the hedge. Chet looked up and tapped my arm.

"Tag, you're it!" Everyone took off, me in hot pursuit until I could tag Lisa, the slowest runner in the group.

As the shadows gathered under the tree, the adults came together on the patio to enjoy their favorite evening drinks and our little gang of kids played croquet, tapping the balls everywhere except through the metal wickets. The women made sure snacks were set out and drink fixings were in place, reminding the server to fill the ice bucket. When Dad and the other men came back from the office, the women called out to them.

"Ax, we're out here. Come and join us," said one of the women. Mom called Dad by his given name, Carroll, but his friends mostly called him Ax, from our last name, Aksamit. They mixed gin and tonics in tall skinny glasses and martinis in stemmed, cone-shaped glasses with imported olives while they shared the news of the day. Conversation ebbed and flowed between excited chatter and intense discussion, but quieted whenever they noticed us kids around. I heard snippets as Mom and Dad talked in hushed tones. They were talking about the war, debating how it was going to end, wondering what was going to happen to all of us. Darkness fell, flashes of light gleamed briefly in the sky, and occasionally the house shuddered. I could hear the drone of fighter planes all night as the Pakistan and Indian Air Forces battled back and forth over the border.

Thinking back to when we had been at our own home, Mom and Dad talked about the war with neighbors and pored over the propaganda-filled newspaper, but it never felt real. Dad's perimeter patrols had become more deliberate, and he'd talk with the night watchman each evening.

"Carroll, we can't hear anything. Is the fighting close? Or are you being paranoid?" Mom had asked as he checked all the doors for the tenth time.

"I don't know. We've been hearing that the Indians are targeting train tracks, and we have those tracks right outside the compound wall."

That night, a low, dull thud woke me. Dad flew down the hallway and ran to the back door. I heard the rat-a-tat-tat sound of gunfire, like I had heard in the movies. I was scared, but I knew Dad would keep us safe. Everything went silent and after a few minutes, Dad closed the back door and checked on me.

"I think the fighting is getting closer, but it seems quiet right now. Go back to sleep and I'll wake you if it starts again." He came over and pulled the covers over me and Chuz and tucked us in. That made me feel better. I tried to stay up to help him listen, because I knew he'd still be up roaming around, but I soon fell asleep.

Dad went to work the next day, but told Mom to stay inside and keep me home from school. "I'm going to see what I can find out," he said.

He came home right after lunch, much earlier than usual. "Dorothy, start packing. We're going to the Warnock's. The fighting is getting too close and a bunch of us are going to stay there because they have the biggest house and they're not near a rail line," Dad said.

Mom packed our bags quickly and we jumped in the car and had the driver whisk us to the Warnocks.

Each day, the men staying at the Warnock's house went to work at the IECo offices, at least for a few hours, coming back with tidbits of information they had gleaned from news reports and colleagues.

I loved being around all the other kids, and the mothers helped each other out. Four families ended up banding together. The cook kept a steady flow of meals going, and cocktails were plentiful. I drank more orange Fanta than would normally be allowed. It was an oddly festive time. Through it all, Mom insisted we spend some productive time each day reading, sewing the dress, and doing problems in my math workbook, even though school was on hold.

When Dad came to tuck me in each night, he told me wonderful stories from when he grew up on the farm in Kansas. He grew quite animated as he spun tales about winter blizzards, riding horses to school with his eight siblings, how all the families had to take turns housing the teacher, and the time he and his brother Leonard rode the rails from Kansas to California and up to Oregon during the Great Depression. But one night, instead of asking him to tell me about Pony Boy, I asked him what the war was about. He thought about it for a moment.

"The Pakistanis and Indians are mad at each other."

"But why?"

"It's complicated, but they are arguing about Kashmir."

"Kashmir? That's where I caught my fish."

I couldn't imagine the peaceful lake being a place of war. But then I remembered how good it felt to catch my colorful fish and how I admired the sun glinting off the shiny scales. And then how bad I felt when I realized what it meant to kill it and steal its soul. Why did everything good have to have something bad associated with it? I wished I could make time go backwards, so I could put the fish back in the water and go home to my room. I wanted everything to be normal again, so I could go to school and play croquet with Chip and swim in Lisa's pool.

"Kashmir is right on the border, and they both want it. You know, Pakistan and India used to be all one country. Now they're fighting like cats and dogs. The Pakistanis thought they could take all of Kashmir, maybe because most people there are Muslim. But India wants to keep it. I know it's confusing."

"Are they killing each other?"

"Yes, unfortunately, people are dying on both sides."

I mulled that over. Kashmir was a special place, and I could understand why they both wanted it. Nothing was worth killing, though. I didn't want to be in this house anymore. I wanted to be in my own bed, in our house. "Can we go home?"

"Not yet. It's too close to the fighting."

"Are we safe here?"

"Yes, of course. If it gets dangerous, the company will make sure we're safe."

"What if they can't?"

"Then the Embassy will make sure we get out. Don't worry. We're safe."

That's all I needed to hear. I snuggled with Chuz under the covers.

EVACUATION

Two weeks later, rumors were flying. The British had already evacuated, and then, one by one, all the other European countries followed suit. I heard the adults wondering why everyone else was gone and the Americans were still here. Most of the fighting was taking place in Kashmir, but the Indian Army was also launching attacks around Lahore. They got so close to the Lahore International Airport that the United States government finally had to request a cease-fire to evacuate US citizens—meaning us—which was granted. It was time to get out.

When the evacuation orders for US citizens finally came, it was only for women and children and Dad had to stay behind. This, despite the possibility of Lahore being surrounded by the Indian Army. We could bring only what we could carry. I watched Mom pack our silver cutlery and her jewelry in one extremely heavy Pan Am shoulder bag I could barely lift, and our clothing in another. She was tense and focused, her mouth drawn into a tight line. I clutched Chuz, the only thing on my list that was non-negotiable. I could have left my troll behind, but luckily, Mom tucked him into one of our suitcases. The adults had spread maps of the Middle East on tables at cocktail hour for the past week as they plotted possible routes back home.

"I thought we'd leave together. Will you be OK here?" Mom asked Dad.

"Sure, we'll be fine. All the men will stay together, and I'm sure the next plane will be for us."

"Do you know where they'll send us?"

"We don't know yet, but probably to the nearest safe country. When you arrive, you can go to a travel agent and arrange your flights to the US."

"Should we wait for you before we continue on?"

"No, because we don't know how long that might be. It's better if you at least get to Europe, but getting to the US is best. You're going to be fine. You made it all the way here from California with Inga when she was only four years old. She's nearly eight now, so it will be easier." He put his arm around her, and they went back to the maps. I wondered how easy it would be.

On the day we left, we heard a honk from a car out in front. Tipton and Kalmbach had organized a car convoy to the airport for safety in numbers, picking up American women and children along the way in a long, snaking row of cars. Mom clung to Daddy for a moment, and I wouldn't let go of his legs, grasping a fold of his pants in my hands, feeling the smooth texture of the fabric. Maybe he could come with us, after all. But he lifted me up for a big hug and kissed my cheek before opening the car door.

"Don't worry, I'll join you and Mom soon."

Stop the car, I wanted to shout, *so we can go back and get Daddy*. I turned around and watched him grow smaller as we pulled away. Mom turned and gave a quick wave, then stared resolutely ahead, wiping her eyes.

We waited restlessly for a long time in the airport and the sun had set before we boarded. The moms milled around, talking to each other about travel plans, everyone trying to figure out how they were going to get back to the US, not knowing if or when the men might be evacuated, while the kids skipped around, burning off energy. By now, we knew we were being evacuated to Tehran, Iran. Mom acted like she knew what she was doing, but I could tell something was off by the tightness in her voice, the forced cheerfulness, and the worry lines around her eyes. It was one thing to set off on a grand adventure to a new land with all kinds of anticipation and suspense, quite another to face this degree of uncertainty.

The airplane sitting on the tarmac looked different from the planes we flew to get to Pakistan. It was a U.S. military C-130 Hercules transport plane, wide and squat, with a big hole for the rear cargo door. We watched men in uniforms going in and out of the cavernous exit onto a wide ramp. When it was our turn to walk from the airport to the plane, we walked up the ramp and saw that it was even less like a typical commercial airplane. There were no comfortable seats with flight attendants or magazines. There were long rows of seats that folded down from the interior walls of the plane, and the floor was metal. Mesh netting lined the walls. Straps and cables hung down everywhere, and equipment was lashed to every surface. There were no seat belts.

My friends, Chet and Lisa, were on the flight, but everyone was quiet in the unfamiliar environment. The chatter dissipated once we boarded. It was eerily quiet. The women sat with their children, every family split in two by having to leave their fathers and husbands behind in the war zone. The gunfire and bombs had been distant, detached from my world, but here, without Daddy, I was scared. I sat still, barely breathing, holding Chuz close with one hand, the other on Mom's leg, my leg pressed against hers. My imaginary friends, Little Boy and Little Girl, hovered over us. We knew we were headed to a safe place, but no one had any idea what would come next. Dad said Mom would figure it out when we got there and not to worry, but looking around at the women's faces, there was plenty of worry. Mom put her arm around my shoulders and held me tight, her body tense, the heavy silver in the Pan Am bag tucked between her feet.

"Everything is going to be okay," she said, as much to herself as to me.

The door closed, and the plane lifted off. We left our home, my school, Dad, and Pakistan far behind.

4

Culture Clash in California

TEHRAN

hen we left Lahore on September 15, 1965, I worried that bullets might strike the underbelly of the plane and hit me, and we'd fall from the sky. When we leveled off, I stopped squirming in my seat, relieved to feel safe in the sky. Our four-hour evacuation flight felt much longer, but we finally landed in inky darkness in Tehran, Iran.

An Iranian family greeted each American family in the blinding light of the airport lobby. I waved goodbye to Lisa and Chet, saying, "See you at school when we get back!"

When the Iranians agreed to take in war refugees, I'm not sure who they were expecting, probably Pakistani evacuees, but it wasn't us middle-class Americans. They were welcoming, if bewildered, and our assigned couple showed us to their comfortable guest room when we arrived at their large, elegant home in an urban neighborhood of the city. They spoke perfect English, and Mom shared details about our escape from Lahore. We didn't know what the next leg of our journey would be, but we were glad to be in a comfortable place for the moment.

The next morning when I woke, Mom was gone. I dressed myself in the clothes I wore the night before and cracked the door open just a hair. I wanted to find Mom, but was wary about leaving the room by myself. The woman of the house appeared and beckoned me to follow her to the sunny, modern kitchen, where she gave me some flat bread with fig jam for breakfast. Tall and slender, with short, dark brown hair, she wore a belted shift dress and low heels like Mom might wear at home. She smiled at me and looked kind, but I felt shy.

"My husband took your mother downtown to run some errands. She will be back soon. Here, please eat something," she said with a smile. "I wish my children were younger, so you'd have someone to play with, but they are grown and living on their own. Here's a picture of them," she said, reaching for a framed photo of a young man and woman standing in a garden. "It's just me and my husband now, so quiet. If you're here for a few days, maybe you can meet the rest of my family."

Tongue-tied, I ate in uncomfortable silence, wondering how long Mom would be gone.

"Would you like to stay here in the kitchen with me?"

"Can I go back to the bedroom?" She led me back and told me to let her know if I needed anything.

I sat on the bed, clutching Chuz close to my chest. My limbs felt wooden, yet my mind was jumpy. Reading didn't calm me because random thoughts kept crowding in. *Mom was coming back, right? What if she didn't?* Little Boy chimed in. *That's ridiculous. She's just running errands,* he said in my imagination. I looked at Chuz and she stared back, clear eyed and steadfast. She never seemed to have any worries. I drew her to me and rocked her, the back-and-forth motion soothing me as I waited.

Mom returned, buzzing with energy. I immediately relaxed as soon as I saw her, my wooden limbs suddenly part of my body again.

"I went to the travel agent, got our tickets to Beirut, Lebanon, and cashed some traveler's checks. Thank goodness. I only had thirty-five American dollars in cash. Whew, I'm glad we have all the flights for the rest of the trip. We leave tonight. Did you know they call Beirut the Paris of the Middle East? I found a nice hotel with a pool, so you can swim."

I smiled at that last part. I wasn't sure what was special about Paris, nor did I know whether thirty-five dollars was a lot or a little. I only knew rupees. However, I loved to swim and that's all I cared about now.

"It's only a few hours to Beirut, but it's a long haul to the States with a several stops. Soon, we'll be back in Texas with Grandma and Grandpa. I sent a telegram to Grandad to let him know," she said.

"Will Dad be there?"

"No, not yet. He's still in Lahore."

I frowned and pointed at the new ring on her finger. "What's that?"

"Oh, there was a jewelry store next to the travel agent. It only took a minute. Isn't it pretty? It's an emerald."

She took the ring off and let me feel the smooth, cool surface of the green stone. I liked it, but I wished I could have gone out with Mom. Why hadn't she taken me with her? And why was she shopping for jewelry when everything was so serious? We had just escaped from the war, we didn't have Daddy with us, and we were staying with strangers. How could she be in the mood for shopping?

"I suppose it was frivolous, but I just needed a little pick-me-up. It was such a rush leaving Lahore and we still have a long journey." She gave me a hug. "But we're on our way now, tickets and cash in hand."

Beirut was wonderful. The pool at the hotel sparkled in the sunlight like diamonds. We were so hot and sweaty by the time we arrived that, even though it was early evening, we went for a delicious swim. I could have stayed in the water for hours. When we drove in from the airport in a taxi, I could see how different Beirut was compared to Lahore or Tehran. There were wide swaths of lush, green parks, lots of trees, and many of the buildings downtown had balconies with curly iron works. Mom loved everything and kept exclaiming over the fashionable western-style dresses and suits she saw other women wearing. She couldn't wait to go shopping and have coffee at one of the outdoor cafes with small tables while I sipped my Coca Cola, a special treat. We could see the blue water of the Mediterranean Sea, and I knew I'd get my pool time each day, so I didn't care what we did as long as I was with Mom.

MEMPHIS

We hopscotched across the Middle East and finally ended up in Memphis. Mom always said that she spent most of her growing-up years plotting how to get out of Texas, but it wasn't such a terrible place. The town was so small that we were minor celebrities just by being there, a diversion from the mundane routines of life for people living on the high plains.

A newspaper reporter interviewed Mom, and our picture was in the paper. I was so used to looking different from Pakistanis. Here, I looked the same as everyone else, yet we were so different that we were featured in the local news. After that, everyone wanted to be my friend at the school Mom enrolled me in.

Bonita, my friend I had met during home leave a couple of years earlier, was in my class at school and wanted to show me how to pick cotton so we could make our own pillow stuffing. I had seen photos of Black families picking cotton with children my age or younger before there were harvesting machines, and I wanted to see what it was like. She brought a pillowcase, and we followed the ruddy red brick road to the edge of town. We snuck between rows of cotton, plucking the fluffy, soft white puffs from the protective hard brown boll. I threw myself into the first row with enthusiasm. We skipped every few plants so it wouldn't be obvious that we were stealing the cotton. By the time I reached the second row, I was hot and sweaty, and my hands were covered with small scrapes from the hard boll. Some of the boll got under my fingernails as I slipped my fingers between the boll and the cotton, and by the time we had enough to stuff the pillowcase, my back was sore. How did they do this all day long? The cotton was lumpy and hard bits of the boll were stuck in some tufts, but we were proud of our accomplishment.

We appeared to be fine, socializing and participating in small town life, but being separated from Dad was taking a toll on both of us. Mom showed me her ring finger. All around her wedding ring was rough, scaly, red skin. It was the only place on her body affected, as if all her worry about Dad coalesced in that one spot on her skin. The finger with the emerald ring was fine.

We tried to settle into a routine while we waited for Dad, but it was hard. I went through each day trying to act normal, but occasionally, a seething anxiety leaked out. Sometimes I got mad easily. Enraged, in fact.

One day, Mom left me overnight with my grandmother to pick Dad up from the airport. We were all excited and relieved to know he was out of the war zone. At first, I was fine. After we went for a walk, I curled up on the sofa and read a book. When Grandma wanted me to take a bath, I resisted, consumed with solving Nancy Drew's *Mystery of the Brass Bound Trunk*.

In this book, Nancy ended up in South America, the first book of the series I had read that was set in another country and I wanted to keep reading. Grandma gently reminded me about the bath after a few minutes. I wasn't mad at first, but suddenly I could feel rage boiling up like a volcano ready to blow. It arrived so fast I couldn't find a way to bring myself down. I yelled that I didn't want to take a bath and when Grandma tried to steer me into the bathroom. I clung to the door. Exasperated, she pried my fingers off the handle and hugged me. I calmed down long enough for her to get me in the tub, but the rage remained.

As soon as Grandma left and closed the door behind her, I beat my fists against the tub, wailing inconsolably between choking breaths. Every time I slowed down, I reminded myself how mad I was and started up again. My diminutive, white-haired grandmother was at her wit's end, alternately trying to calm me, soothe me, leave me alone, scold me, and tempt me with food, ice cream, and Dr. Pepper. She tried everything she could think of. I wasn't having any of it. I wanted my mom. No one else would do.

In the bathtub, I howled at the top of my lungs until the water was ice cold. Snot and salty tears mixed with the bathwater as I blubbered, "I want my mommy," over and over. There were no words to describe my deep well of emptiness and no way to understand my feelings. Finally, I emerged from the tub, crying tears of fury and despair into the towel. After snuffling my way through putting on my pajamas, I cracked open the door, still weeping, and looked at Grandma. She tried to reach out to me, but I went into the bedroom and crawled into bed with wet hair.

"Do you want any dinner?" Grandma asked.

I blubbered into the sheets.

"I don't know what to do. Your mother will be back tomorrow. She just went to the airport in Amarillo to pick up your father. Come and get me if you want anything," she said as she closed the door. I sobbed into the pillow before falling asleep, totally exhausted.

The morning after the tantrum, I awoke with my shoulder-length, thick brown hair in a snarl. I dragged a brush through it, which tamed it only slightly. Grandma and I were wary of each other. I was ashamed and didn't understand what was happening or how to bridge the divide between us. I was eight years old—way too old to be throwing tantrums of that magnitude.

Grandma made a couple of futile attempts at communication and then gave up after getting monosyllabic responses from me, then bustled around the wood-paneled kitchen getting my breakfast. "You must be hungry after not having any dinner," she said, plunking down a big plate of fried eggs, bacon, and white toast. I looked down at my plate and nibbled at the edges, not hungry. After breakfast, I went downstairs to read my book. The storm cellar was furnished with sofas and beds for when the winds blew so hard that sirens screamed at a high pitch to warn of tornados. I moved the protective plastic covering off the sofa and made a little nest for myself so I could read my book in peace.

I wasn't in the mood to solve mysteries, so I moved to something closer to home. I lost myself in A Little Princess, a story about an English girl born in India who was sent to boarding school by her father for her education. She was a little girl like me, and I hoped Dad wouldn't die like the girl's father. I remembered how the servants *salaamed* to us, touching their forehead with their hands, and called Dad *sahib* like her father. The carved teakwood furniture and wool rugs with intricate designs that Sara described were familiar, as were the simple furnishings in the storm cellar that were like the plain attic Sara was sent to live after her father died.

When I heard the car pull up to the back door, I flew out to see Dad. Bending down to give me a bear hug after prying my arms from around his legs, he said, "There's my best girl. Oh, how I missed you." The smell of his familiar All-Spice aftershave made me weak in the knees with relief that he was home. I had been so keyed up since Mom left, but now I felt like I could sleep for days with all of us safely together. Even though Grandma had told me he was coming, I hadn't believed it until I saw him in person. Thank goodness he didn't die like Sara's father. I sidled up to Mom and breathed easier when she held me tight. She didn't know how bad I had been the night before.

I kept a close watch on my grandmother during all the greetings to see if I was going to get in trouble like Sara did in the book. Grandma must have gotten Mom alone when I didn't notice because eventually Mom asked me what had happened. "I don't know," I mumbled. "I thought you weren't coming back."

"Of course, I was coming back. I just had to go get Daddy. You knew that." She didn't get mad at me, which surprised me. "I'm sorry I left you with Grandma. It's been hard on all of us, but we're together again. Go on out there and be with your daddy."

Later, when things settled down, Dad came to tuck me in. I asked him how he got out of Pakistan. "Did they send the big military plane for you like ours?"

"No, not exactly. I'll tell you about it tomorrow. We all need to get some sleep first," he said. He gave me a kiss on the cheek and turned the lights out.

The next day, Dad got grandad's globe out and showed me how he got out of Pakistan. We traced the line together on the round, bumpy ball. "A few weeks after you and Mom left, we understood that there wasn't going to be an evacuation for the men. All the diplomats were evacuated, but people who worked for private companies, like me, were on their own. I scrambled to get visas and figured out how to leave. There was too much fighting near the airport, so I couldn't fly out. I went through Afghanistan. Remember me talking about Afghanistan?" I waited a moment to answer because I was still stuck on no plane for the men. How did the company expect them to get out? Were they just going to leave them there? Things had been worse for Dad than I thought.

"Yes. You used to work there before you met Mom," I said after I caught up. Dad had worked in the Helmand Valley in Afghanistan for four years in the mid-1950s on the Morrison Knudsen project, one of the first well-meaning but misguided U.S.-based projects designed to "fix" Afghanistan, a legacy that continues to this day. At that time, King Zahir Shah of Afghanistan wanted to turn the desert into an oasis through the miracle of irrigation. But the soil was salty, the fields didn't drain as expected, and after twelve years of effort, the project ultimately failed.

"That's right. First, I took the train to Rawalpindi. His finger traced the line that separated Pakistan from Afghanistan. "The cook made me a big box full of food with roast beef sandwiches, potato salad, and ice cream." He paused for effect.

"Ice cream?" I asked, my mouth agape. That was so funny, but not surprising since our cook sometimes did silly things that didn't make sense. I missed him and the mango slices he used to give me.

He laughed. "You've guessed the problem! The sandwiches were swimming in melted ice cream by the time I got to them. I had to throw most of it out. I got some kebabs and chapatti when we stopped in Rawalpindi."

"How did you cross the border?"

"I took another train from Rawalpindi to Peshawar near the border. I hired a car and driver to get from Peshawar to the Afghanistan border.

It only took about thirty minutes. I told the driver I needed to get a ride in Afghanistan to Kabul, but I wasn't sure how I'd find another driver. When I got through customs, a driver materialized in front of me like magic and showed me to a car. It was about four hours to Kabul over the Khyber Pass. I stayed there one night and then flew to Kandahar, where the Morrison Knudsen office used to be. That was a relief, since I knew my way around. I even saw a friend from the old job site. From there I flew to Beirut."

What a complicated journey. I thought it was hard for me and Mom, but this was worse. At least he got to Beirut.

"That's where Mom and I stopped, too!"

We spun the globe around a few times while I absorbed his story.

"Who won the war?" I asked after a few minutes.

"It's hard to say; maybe no one. They each lost a few thousand soldiers, and they are still sharing Kashmir, so it might be a draw—a whole lot of hullaballoo over nothing. They've been arguing over Kashmir for a long time, and I'm not sure this skirmish settled anything. Pakistan used to be part of India and a lot of people died when the British imposed Partition. I don't think they've moved on from that. And China is over on the other side—who knows if they got involved, too. I'm just glad we're out of there."

"When will we go back? I'm supposed to start third grade." It didn't sound like it was worth it to go to war and kill a bunch of people over Kashmir. But I was interested in what would happen to me.

"I don't think we will. It's near the end of my contract, so we'll head back to California. We'll find you a new school."

That shook me up, and I needed some time to think about what he said. I thought Dad would come to get us, we'd travel around like we did before, then we'd go home, back to my school and friends. But now home was going to be in California. I'd never see my room again, or my school, or my friends.

"What about your work project in Lahore? What will happen to that?"

"I'm not sure, but it might just end, or maybe they'll send another team out to re-start it."

"Will we go back to Vacaville?" I asked. I barely remembered Vacaville after four years.

"I don't know. I'll see where they need me. I've sent some letters out already. Some people I worked with in Afghanistan and Vacaville are still in California. Hopefully, I'll be able to line something up in a different country, but if I find work in California, we'll stay there for a bit. My buddies will keep an eye out and let me know if they hear of overseas jobs."

"Really? Is that how it works?"

"Yes, it's not just what you know, it's who you know. You remember Mr. Maestes? We worked together in Afghanistan. He's the one who told me about the position in Pakistan. There are not that many people who like to live in other countries, so we share information about those positions. Once I got a taste for travel after being in the South Pacific in World War II, I was hooked. In fact, I met a guy on Wake Island during the war who had been in a Japanese prisoner-of-war camp. Turns out, he had been working for Morrison Knudsen on Wake Island when they were building an airstrip, and all the workers were captured by the Japanese. I was bowled over when he picked me up from the airport in Karachi when I moved to Afghanistan for Morrison Knudsen. Can you imagine? I knew a random guy in the war, and I ran into him working in Afghanistan?"

I couldn't imagine. After Dad tucked me in, I thought about Chet and Lisa. Where were they? Would I ever see them again? I was sorry I hadn't said more to them when we were at the airport in Tehran. My mind raced as I ticked off more and more people I'd miss. Was it possible I'd never see my teacher again? My classmates? And what about my things—my comic book collection and croquet set? And my bedroom where I had everything just so? I hugged Chuz extra tight that night. At least I still had Chuz.

HANFORD

After a quick visit to Kansas to see Dad's family, we were on our way back to California. Dad got a job as a consultant in Hanford, California, a rural town near Fresno, with Stoddard and Karrer. This was the same company he worked for before we went to Lahore, which he landed through a connection he made with one of the owners in Afghanistan. This job was an irrigation project near Tulare Lake in the San Joaquin Valley. We moved there from Texas just as my finger started to fester. It throbbed with the piece of cotton boll that was stuck under my fingernail from the time I picked cotton with Bonita.

"Looks like it's getting infected. We'd better get some Mercurochrome on it," said Dad, peering at the end of my index finger. When he painted the orange antiseptic on the cut, the wound stung and I yelped, pulling my finger away.

"It looks like it's right under your fingernail. I'd better keep an eye on this," Dad said.

Two days later, my finger was swollen and red, so Mom bundled me off to the doctor's office in one of my best plaid suspender skirts and a crisply pressed white blouse. She wore a pale blue dress with a tight bodice and flared skirt, cinched at the waist, and matching pumps. Going to the doctor's office was an event to get dressed up for.

The doctor removed the bandage and looked carefully at my finger. "How long has it been like this?" he asked.

"About a week," Mom said.

The doctor squeezed my finger gently. White pus oozed out of the wound.

"It's pretty swollen. We need to remove the fingernail and let it drain," he said. *Take the finger off? Did I hear that right?* That sounded bad. I fought back tears.

"Mom, I'm scared. Are they going to cut my finger off?" I asked when we got back in the car, unable to hold the tears back.

"No, silly. Just your fingernail. They'll numb your finger with medicine, and I'll be with you the whole time," she said. That made me feel a little better, but I snuffled all the way home.

The next day, the nurses at the Catholic hospital asked Mom to wait in the waiting room, but she insisted on coming into the tiled procedure room.

"Please stand against the wall," they instructed Mom.

I whimpered when they gave me the injections at the base of my finger to numb it, but I kept my eyes on Mom. They positioned a bright light over my finger and the doctor went to work. I tried to stay very still, but it startled me to hear a light clink followed by a loud crash. I looked over, but Mom was gone.

The nurse yelled, "We need help!"

Another nurse rushed to the other side of the room and bent over Mom. "She's breathing. I think she fainted," she said. Mom had passed out, hitting her head on the tiled wall when she saw the doctor lift off my fingernail. She came to and was given a quick escort out of the procedure room to lie down while she absorbed the news from the doctor. The infection had penetrated my bone in a condition known as osteomyelitis. She told me later that she had seen the end of my bone fall out onto the stainless-steel tray and that's when she fainted.

Mom was woozy and had a bump on her head while I didn't feel a thing until later that night when the local anesthetic wore off. Worse for me were the twice-a-day intramuscular injections of antibiotics into my bottom.

The daily injections became a battleground. I screamed and raged every morning and afternoon at the clinic. Mom gradually lost patience. The only person who could calm me was Sister Angelica, a plump, motherly nun, dressed in a severe habit of white robes, a starched white wimple around her face and black veil. Her wooden rosary beads hung from her waist. She worked some kind of voodoo magic to soothe my frayed nerves every day. One day, she was off duty and another nun tried to give me the injection. When I shrieked, Mom tried to hold me still and nurses grabbed my arms and legs to hold me down. The banshee in me came out, kicking and biting and scratching.

Mom shouted, "Stop" over the mayhem, and everyone let go of my writhing body. "We need to figure out a different way," she said, stroking my head as I curled up in the fetal position. The nurses huddled to come up with a new plan. Suddenly, Sister Angelica appeared, summoned by a call from the nurses. She sent everyone out of the room, including Mom, and held me close against her ample bosom while I cried. She spoke softly and eventually asked if I was ready. I let her give me the shot. The intense shame I felt at creating such a scene and disturbing the kind Sister on her day off overwhelmed me. It was that same rage that happened with the grandma tantrum that I couldn't control. I would be feeling fine and then it was like a bee buzzing deep inside trying to get out, and in an instant I became a monster.

Sister Angelica was there for the rest of the injections and on the last day, she gave me a black-and-white photograph of her playing the guitar, which I treasured for many years. I never forgot what a soothing, calming presence she was, like love personified. I felt like she could see inside my soul and no matter what I did, she would never judge me or give up on me.

Dad came home every night after work, kissed me on the cheek, and examined my finger carefully. "It's looking better," he said. "I'm relieved. I know it's hard on you getting the shots, but you need the medicine to help you get better. There was an infection in the bone and the antibiotics are important."

"I know, Daddy. I'll try to do better."

"It's ok. You're not doing anything bad, but when you get so upset, it's hard on Mom. It makes it harder on you. And even Sister Angelica. Try to be brave." He patted my arm and smoothed my mussed hair back from my face. "The important thing is that you're getting better. The shots will end soon, I promise."

I didn't know why I was so angry and out of control. The injections were painful for a moment, but the pain didn't last long. All the uncertainty and tension from the war and being without Dad for so many months concentrated in these twice-a-day events. It was confusing.

My fingernail eventually grew back, but it was thicker and more rounded than my others, and my left index finger was noticeably shorter than my right since part of the bone had fallen off in surgery. The doctor said I was lucky I didn't lose my whole finger.

So much for being a cotton picker.

* * *

When school started, Mom took me in for a meeting with the principal and a couple of teachers. The grassy campus had extensive fields and several long, low buildings with classrooms that all had outside entrances.

"She's a bit young for third grade," the principal said.

My mother was steadfast. "Yes, we started her a year early because we knew we'd be moving around indefinitely. Her schooling might get disrupted. In fact, at the end of second grade, we had to leave Pakistan earlier than expected," Mom said.

The principal examined the report card Mom had brought. "What is Urdu? I see her grade was 'Unsatisfactory' but that it improved by the last grading period."

"It's the language of Pakistan. It was part of the curriculum."

They decided that testing was necessary to place me in the correct grade. The fake smiles were intended to reassure me, but there was tension in the room. Mom looked nervous. I remembered hearing about those kids who lost a year because they moved around a lot. I didn't mind taking tests, but instantly felt the pressure. They put me in a room by myself with the testing booklet. I worked my way through the math and reading comprehension questions the way I always did, rarely going back to questions I knew I didn't know the answer to.

"Done already?" They seemed surprised, but took the papers to another room for grading. I started to worry. Maybe I should have checked my answers. Just as I was breaking into a sweat, they came in and said I could join the third grade. I breathed a sigh of relief and Mom relaxed. All the smiles were real now.

On the first day of school, my teacher called roll. "Betty As ... Aks ... AkSAM ... Betty, how do you pronounce your last name?"

"My name is Inga," I said.

"But it says here that your name is Betty."

"I go by Inga. It's my middle name. And my last name is AK-sa-mit," I said, emphasizing the first syllable and sounding them all out.

By now, all eyes were staring at me, and I felt my face flush.

"Class, Inga's family just moved here, so please show her around at recess."

I stared at the ground while roll call continued.

At recess, one kid came up and asked me where I was from.

"Pakistan," I said.

"Where's that? I've never heard of it."

"It's far away."

"Want to play tetherball?" They clearly didn't have any interest in knowing where Pakistan was.

"I don't know how."

"You don't know how? Everyone plays tetherball. I'll show you." I felt stupid for not knowing what tetherball was, but grateful that the kids showed me how. One kid made fun of me every time I didn't hit the ball or duck fast enough, and it banged into my head. Mom took me to the school playground on the weekend so I could practice without the kids laughing at me and eventually I got better. Everything was different. There was no croquet. My name was different, I didn't know what to say about where I was from, and I didn't know how to play the games. At least I made it into third grade without losing a year. I understood now what that meant, and I didn't want to ever lose a year.

SAN FRANCISCO

A year later, we were in a temporary apartment in San Francisco after dad's consulting job ended in Hanford. He was back with Morrison Knudsen, the company he worked for in Afghanistan, now in a subsidiary called International Engineering Company, which everyone called IECo. Each job resulted in more contacts, and he kept getting job offers and referrals from an ever-widening circle of colleagues in the international irrigation circle.

Alamo Elementary School was different from Hanford. It was an urban school with two stories and a main entrance facing the sidewalk in front. I was struck by the tall rectangular windows in the classrooms that tilted open from the top. There was a wide staircase in the middle and all the doors to the classrooms were inside, along either side of a large hallway. The asphalt playground was in the back of the classrooms, with a chain-link fence between the play area and sidewalk. The entire school fit between 22nd and 23rd Avenues, taking up half the block.

Roll call on the first day of school was about the same as Hanford and, as always, Aksamit came first. "Betty Aska ... AkSAM ... how do you say your name?"

"My name is Inga," I said. And we repeated the entire sequence, practically word for word, until the teacher sorted out my first and last names.

They were just starting to cover what I had already done in grammar, but there were some sections I wasn't familiar with because I missed them in the previous year. There were also some gaps in math. I was a whiz with multiplication and division, but I never learned to add or subtract quickly in my head. I plowed forward, reading everything I could get my hands on at the neighborhood library while I squeaked along in math. My report cards reflected reality with A grades in some subjects, average grades in math, and the usual comments about being a "social butterfly" and "could do better with less talking with her classmates."

At recess, I was relieved to see a tetherball pole, the game I was now proficient in, but I was disappointed to see that in this school, tetherball was played by the younger kids. Most of the kids in my grade were playing hopscotch on white lines painted on the asphalt. Thanks to a friend who lived in our apartment building who had taught me how to draw big squares on the sidewalk with chalk, I had a head start with hopscotch and I quickly learned four square, a new game for me. I knew by now that I had to learn the games quickly to make friends and fit in. That was more important than math.

After a few months, we moved to a stucco house on 47th Avenue in a nicer neighborhood. The house had three bedrooms sitting on top of the garage and a big backyard. We were close to Land's End, a magical place on a large bluff where we could look out at the Pacific Ocean, Marin Headlands, and Golden Gate Bridge. The stubby Mile Rocks lighthouse close to Land's End lulled me to sleep at night with its low, comforting, baritone foghorn. We were only a couple of blocks from the Great Highway and often took picnics to the enormously long sandy beach, even on cold, foggy summer days when the water was steely gray. I was captivated by the steady rhythm of the waves rolling gently to the shore. I imagined their long journey from Japan crossing the vast expanse of sea to lap at my feet.

Although our new house was only fifteen blocks from our previous apartment, it meant I was assigned to a different school. I transferred to Lafayette Elementary School, a three-story building that looked like it was built from the same blueprint as Alamo Elementary School. The name game started again on the first day of class. "Betty," Miss Lee said. I wanted to say, "Stop right there," but I politely waited for her first attempts before I said, all in a rush this time, "I go by Inga, my middle name, and my last name is AK-sa-mit." I grew to like Miss Lee very much. She was kind, and I felt comfortable around her.

"Did you just move here? Where are you from?" a girl from my class asked at recess. I had a moment of panic. *Where was I from? Hanford? Pakistan? Texas? Vacaville?*

"Uh, Pakistan. We moved around a lot," I mumbled.

Her eyes lit up. "My parents moved here from Hong Kong, but I was born in San Francisco. My Chinese name is Li, but I go by Lisa. I could relate when you had to tell Miss Lee you went by a different name. I have to do that every year, too."

"I've been to Hong Kong!" I exclaimed, a big smile spreading across my face as I sensed a connection with her.

"I'm jealous. I'd love to go to Hong Kong. Maybe someday. Let's play a game."

Most of the kids in my class were black-haired children with family names such as Yamamoto, Nakamura, or Wong. There were only a few kids who looked like me, but I was used to that. In Pakistan, the kids in school were mostly Westerners, while people on the street were South Asian. Here, most of my classmates were Asian. I admired the kids with Japanese lunches made of rice and small bits of meat and vegetables, all arranged in a pretty design, but I was attached to my baloney sandwiches on white bread with yellow mustard. Mom kept asking if I wanted ham or turkey or peanut butter. "Nope, just the usual." I had never had baloney before, so it was an exotic lunch meat for me.

One day, Miss Lee showed us a black-and-white film in class that detailed the lives of school-aged children in Japan. I had visited Japan twice by then and was riveted. *So that's what was going on behind all those closed doors of schools and homes that we had passed in Tokyo.* The film showed the smiling school children, dressed in identical uniforms, reciting their lessons, doing their homework, eating with chopsticks, and going to the market with their mothers. Their lunch meals looked like the ones I saw the Japanese kids eating in our lunchroom. I wanted to go there again and get to know the parts of Japan that I hadn't seen before.

One Saturday, Mom said, "Get ready for a little adventure." That sounded ominous because she said it a little too brightly. We walked a block to the public bus stop on Geary Boulevard. When we boarded, she gave me some coins and showed me how to drop them in the coin box. We traveled ten blocks to 37th Avenue. When we got off, we walked past the Anza Library where I got all my books each week and we were at my school. "That was easy, wasn't it?" said Mom.

"Yes, easy," I said, not thinking much of it.

"Do you think you could do it by yourself? You're nine years old. That should be old enough to take the bus, don't you think?"

I balked. That felt like something entirely different.

"I guess so," I said, feeling a little off balance. So that's what this was all about.

"On Monday, we'll do it again together. You'll be a pro within a week," she said.

We took the bus back home, and I craned my neck to catch the glimpses of ocean views I knew were coming. We were high above the ocean, and I loved seeing the neat rows of houses in their linear forms contrasting with the big, cobalt blue expanse of sparkling ocean stretching to Japan, where all those children were doing their lessons. By now, I had a globe of my own that one of my mother's friends gave me for my birthday and I could spin it around to remind myself of all the places I had been. If I drew a straight line from San Francisco, I'd run right into Japan. I could even trace a line from Japan through the South China Sea, Indian Ocean, and Arabian Sea to Pakistan. On my globe, it didn't seem so far away. I wondered what Chet and Lisa were doing and whether they were back in Lahore.

A few days later, after Mom and I did another practice run, I set off by myself. I sat near the bus driver and was on high alert the whole time, counting each block, reading the street numbers as we lumbered along. With relief, I saw my stop before it was time, pulled the cord, and stepped off. I walked the block to school and felt extremely grown up when I approached the gate by myself. From then on, I got myself back and forth to school, gradually relaxing as I learned the timing and cadence of the journey.

I lived an entire year in San Francisco and although I went to two schools, I felt like I fit in. After school let out, Mom and I embarked on another voyage, this time by sea. Dad had already left to get everything ready for us at our new home in South America. I was sad I wouldn't see Miss Lee or my classmates again, but I had always known we'd be going somewhere sometime. Everybody in Pakistan and many of my classmates in San Francisco were used to moving around to different countries. San Francisco didn't feel as much like home as Lahore had, so I was ready to make new friends in Peru. I never anticipated how difficult it might be, but 1967 was to be a year of many changes for me.

5

Troubled Waters
in Peru

SHIP

om cooked up an unusual plan for our trip to Peru. As before, Dad left early to find housing for us in Piura, a small town in northern Peru where he would work on the San Lorenzo Drainage Project, while Mom finished packing for our two-year stay. Our time in South America would find each of us living in our own world—living together but experiencing Peru in vastly different ways.

Like our journey to Pakistan, Mom created an adventure for us, this time by sea. It wasn't a luxury cruise, though; it was a freighter. We set sail from San Francisco right after I finished fourth grade and headed south to Callao, the port of Lima, Peru.

I was excited to have the first passport of my own, instead of being part of Mom's. For the passport photo, I wore my favorite outfit, a red and white seersucker dress with a matching short-sleeved jacket adorned with four red embroidered strawberries on the front. My shoulder-length honey brown hair was pulled back with a wide headband, and I was smiling.

We were barely settled into our cabin when Mom hustled us onto the deck as we steamed under the Golden Gate Bridge on a bright, clear morning with no fog, huddled against each other to ward off the chill. Looking up at the mighty girders of the bridge, the sun glinting off the brick red paint, we waved goodbye to the city. The Mile Rocks Lighthouse, Seal Rock, and Lands' End that we knew so well from land, now looked so different as we sailed away on the big cargo-laden ship to our new home.

The walls and railings around the small passenger deck were painted white, and wooden lounge chairs with blue and cream striped cushions looked inviting—the metal folding chairs less so. There were a few cabins for paying customers for the two-week journey. It was a jovial bunch except for one reclusive older woman, an author who rarely emerged from her stateroom. Taking a freighter was an uncommon way to travel, and the first evening, over cocktails for the adults and an orange Fanta for me, everyone took turns explaining how they got there.

"It was the cheapest way I could get down to South America—like a poor man's cruise," said Joe, a man with gray hair and a pot belly.

"I hate to fly, and this seemed fun. I'm recently divorced and needed to get away," said Helen as she tucked some flyaway strands of blond hair behind her ear.

When it got to Mom, I was curious to hear what she'd say. What happened to the five-star hotels we stayed in when we moved to Pakistan? It was decidedly basic on the ship.

"It seemed like the most adventurous way to travel and the idea of sailing under the Golden Gate bridge was terribly romantic. I wanted to do something different," she said.

"But you're meeting your husband for a job—wouldn't the company pay for a flight and classy hotel?"

"Sure, but we did that years ago in Japan, and the thought of traveling like that bores me now. It's not real. I don't want to travel in a protected bubble anymore. I want to do things that are outside the lines. It feels like things are changing and women have more freedom. In the '50s, it seemed like there was a formula I had to follow about how to dress and how to be a housewife. But it's 1967 and there's an entire world of possibilities. Isn't this the Summer of Love? That's what they're calling it in San Francisco."

"Yeah, the world is changing, but are the men? I'm surprised your husband would let you," said Joe.

"Let me?" She was indignant. "He was happy with the plan. He doesn't care how we get down to Peru and we can pocket the money we saved from the stipend." She softened. "And he supports me being able to grow and explore. Thank goodness for that."

"That calls for a toast. Here's to Dorothy, the adventurer," said Helen, as the group clinked glasses and Mom beamed at her new honorific. I guess we were adventurers now. I didn't know what the Summer of Love was, but I had seen the hippies in Golden Gate Park.

The rest of the passengers and crew doted on me as I was the lone child on the ship. Both the captain and first mate took a particular liking to me. The middle-aged captain, who had a stocky build and short brown hair, toured me and Mom around the bridge and his quarters. His khaki pants and white collared shirt fit snugly, his rotund waist protruding over his belt. He always looked the same. He invited Mom and me to see his quarters, saying it was nice to have a youngster around for the long voyage. Leaving his door open, he showed us his rooms, including a sitting area with a large table, and he gave us a Coke to share. A logbook, navigation charts, and a large desk calendar were neatly stacked on the table.

"Inga, take a look at my calendar. Every day I mark off one of these big squares, so I know what day it is. Like this," he said as he drew an X in a box for the day. "Come by tomorrow and we can do it together." The next day, when Mom and I dropped by, he handed me the marker.

"Would you like to draw the X today?" Of course I did. I carefully drew the lines and replaced the thick cap. I knew it was a treat that I was allowed to do this, and I showed up every day to mark the calendar. He never asked the other passengers to these off-limits parts of the ship, although he socialized with everyone at dinner.

The first mate came around on the second afternoon to ask Mom if it was all right for me to join him on a tour of the engine room. She looked pleased and said, "Yes," right away. I felt special to get so much attention from a senior member of the crew who took me around to different parts of the ship every day. He was tall and lean with thick black glasses and he always wore matching khaki pants and untucked short-sleeved shirts. We saw flying fish and dolphins off the deck, while in the hold, gigantic pieces of equipment made tremendous metallic clanking sounds. He held my hand as we threaded our way through narrow passageways into the interior of the ship and cautioned me to not look at or speak to the crew, which he referred to as "bad men", below decks. It was a nice way to break up the long days. I was happy to put my book down and join him for the special tours just for me.

"I have something to show you. Have you even seen nautical charts?" he asked, inviting me into his quarters. His room was like the captain's, but unlike the captain, he shut the door when we were inside. He seated me on his lap while he showed me his charts spread out on the large table, pointing out our route while he rubbed my arm. Then he put his hand under my shirt and rubbed my tummy. His wandering hands caught me by surprise, especially when he rubbed my flat chest.

After it happened again on another field trip, I tried to redirect the hands by wearing fitted shirts he couldn't get into. That backfired when he changed tactics and slid his hands up my skirt. Shorts helped if I wore the right top, but he persisted, rubbing my stomach and trying to coax me into taking naps. I had never been a napper and had no interest. I didn't like his hands all over me, but I didn't want to lose the special field trips. Him touching me made me nervous, and I couldn't relax when we were in his room. I thought I might get in trouble if I said something to

Mom, so I kept quiet.

One day, sitting at his desk, he said, "Want to take a nap?"

"No, thanks. I'm not tired."

"I'm tired. I was up all night dealing with a problem on the ship. How about if we rest?"

"I can go back to Mom. I know how to find my way."

"No, I can't let you do that. What if you got lost? Let's rest a few minutes and then I'll take you back." I was trapped. I knew this was wrong and that he was a bad man, but I couldn't think of how to turn it around. He coaxed me to lie down. His hands were everywhere, seemingly disconnected from a body. All the while, my mind grew smaller and smaller until it was the size of a raisin, all my energy concentrated into a tiny black space away from here, away from my body. It didn't matter what happened to my body, I was far away.

Suddenly, there was a knock. He froze. My mind snapped back into my body. There was another knock, this time louder and more urgent. A male voice called his name. He placed a finger across his lips and whispered "shhh." After the third knock, there was the sound of receding footsteps. He waited a moment, then rolled off the bed and threw my clothes at me. "Let's go. I'd better get you back. Don't say anything, OK? This will be our little secret." Just like that, in the space of minutes, I became a nine-year-old girl with a secret.

I flew off the bed, suddenly energized by the realization that I could escape. Emotions trickled in. I was shaking inside but averted my eyes and looked straight ahead like a robot. I ran up the stairs ahead of him and he turned back. Throwing myself into the chaise lounge next to Mom, I panted from the exertion.

"Back so soon? What did you see today?"

"Not much. More of the same." I tried to sound calm. How could I stop this? I struggled between wanting the attention and having to tell him I couldn't go with him anymore. Wouldn't Mom be suspicious? "I'm going to get my book." In our cabin, I sat on the bed and thought about what to do. He didn't really hurt me, did he? Maybe it wasn't so bad.

If I told Mom, she might have a fit and complain to the captain. That would be so embarrassing and then everyone would know. And the first mate would get in trouble after being so nice to me. The field trips were pleasant, but not the wandering hands. The solution was simple. I'd tell him I couldn't go next time he came around. Would that work?

A couple of days later, while I read a book and let my skin roast to a golden brown, the passengers hatched a plan to have a party. Cocktail hour on the deck was popular at the end of every day, but for this event they talked the cook into making appetizers and everyone dressed up. It was warm, and we all enjoyed watching the sunset shading into the endless expanse of blue ocean. That night, everyone took turns singing, reciting poetry, or playing charades. I read knock-knock jokes from my joke book. They wanted the recluse to join the festivities and one by one, different passengers knocked on her cabin door. There was no answer.

"Inga, you should go," said one of the passengers.

"I don't think so. She won't answer."

"You should go because you're a child. Surely, she won't be so rude as to not answer the door." I looked at Mom and she shrugged.

"It might work," she said.

I walked toward her room, preparing my speech. I knocked, not expecting much. To my surprise, the door opened and a tall, slender, stern woman with gray hair pulled neatly into a bun stood before me. I gaped at her but said brightly in my best adult voice, "We're having a party and we'd love for you to join us."

"That's terribly kind of you. Please tell the others that I appreciate it, but I have too much to do," she said.

"Pleeeaase. I'd really like it if you would come for a little bit," I said. I was confident that she would agree because I was used to getting my way.

"No, I can't. I'm working on a book, and I can't get distracted." She closed the door. Crestfallen, I had to return to the group and admit defeat.

* * *

As we sailed closer to Lima, there was an air of excitement when we started seeing seabirds and there was a noticeable increase in crew activity as they readied the boat for our port entry. The kind captain had some snacks and drinks for Mom and me in his cabin to celebrate us marking the last day of the trip on the calendar together. He handed the marker to me, and I made the marks with a flourish, followed by a cheer as we clinked our glasses, mine filled with Coca Cola and theirs with cold beer.

When the First Mate came by to take me around, I said, "I'm too busy packing, but thank you anyway."

Mom overheard me. "Are you sure you don't want to go one last time? He's been so nice to you."

"No, not today," I said, thankful that she didn't pursue it. I was vigorously avoiding him, marking off the days in my head when I would never have to see him again. The passengers had a grand party with champagne and the cook made special appetizers and festive party foods. We could see the faint outline of land for the first time in many days. I could hardly sleep that night, bouncing out of bed at first light. Mom laid out our best traveling clothes, so we'd look nice when Dad picked us up.

As we drew near the harbor, the engines slowed. Something was wrong. The pilot boat wasn't there to greet us, and after several hours, the celebratory tone waned. As the day dragged on, we wondered what was happening. It turned out there was a scheduling issue. The captain had sent a ship-to-shore radio message indicating our arrival date by looking at "our" calendar and somehow, we were a full day early. Apparently, there was some mix-up with how the dates had been marked on the calendar. It's bad form to arrive a day early, resulting in citations and fines for the captain, mass confusion at the dock, and it created an awkward extra night for the passengers after the party was supposed to be over. I felt bad for the captain. He did not look happy.

Mom kept asking me questions. "Did you ever mark the calendar when the captain wasn't there?"

"Of course not."

"Did you ever mark two boxes at once?"

"No!" I was indignant. She seemed to think that I was responsible, but I wasn't buying it. I was a kid following the lead of the captain, with no understanding of the consequences of our game. I had been so careful about drawing the X each day. But could I have accidentally drawn an extra X? Or could he have made a mistake and drawn one after me? How could I know for sure? It shocked me that such a simple thing could have so many consequences. I put it out of my mind. There was enough for me to do to keep the wandering hands at bay without taking on the responsibility for the scheduling mess. There's only so much a nine-year-old can take.

We had a joyful reunion with dad the following day, though there were plenty of whispers on the side as Mom tried to explain what happened. I glared at her, trying to protect my position of innocence in the scheduling matter.

We spent a couple of days sightseeing in Lima. Those went by in a blur of ornate old buildings surrounding a large plaza before we flew, full of anticipation, to our new home base in Piura, over 600 miles to the north. My secret with the bad man was safely tucked away in a little box and I'd never have to think about it again.

PIURA

"Dad, Mom has been telling me about the Incas and Machu Picchu up in the mountains. Will we be near there?"

"No, it won't be anything like that, but we'll visit Machu Picchu someday. We're going north to the Sechura Desert, so it's hot and dry. Piura is close to the equator in Ecuador. In fact, they call Piura the *ciudad del eterno calor*, the city of eternal heat."

"The equator—we learned about that last year. Can we go to the equator?" I was enthralled with the idea of standing on the line where the earth bulged out the furthest.

"Maybe. I hadn't thought about going there."

"How hot is it?" Mom asked.

"It's hot, especially out at the project. When it gets bad, we can escape to the beach. It's an hour away."

"Beach—that means swimming." Peru was sounding better and better to me. Incas, the equator, and beaches.

The heat smacked us in the face when we stepped off the plane. It felt like the blast you get from opening the oven door too fast. From the airport, Dad took us through the downtown area before heading to the house.

"It's such a charming city," said Mom.

"There's a lot of Spanish architecture, so there are some gracious buildings and statues around the plaza. It's very old. The Spanish explorer, Pizarro, established it in the 1500s." Dad pointed at an ornate building across from the town square.

We entered a pleasant neighborhood cooled by big leafy trees lining the street, one in front of each house. As we drove up and parked, my excitement left me breathless. I couldn't wait to see what our next house would look like. The two-story white building looked promising behind a picket fence, corralling an unruly garden in front of our corner lot.

"Oh, Carroll, it looks darling, much nicer than I expected after how you described the housing," Mom said, her eyes sparkling.

"We had a slight change in plans. I'll tell you about it later." The house was smaller than others on the street and it was so close to our neighbor's house that there was no space between them. It had clean, straight lines, metal framed windows, and doors that contained many small panes of glass. In fact, there were forty panes of glass in the front door. Mom and I walked through the house, her heels clicking on the tile floors.

"Interesting floor design," Mom said evenly, disguising any dismay she might have felt about how to decorate with a giant black and white tile chessboard on the floor. I loved the vibrant design, hopscotching my way to the back door, my long, braided pigtails flopping up and down.

The entire back wall consisted of the same small panes of glass as the front door. Mom stepped through the back door into an enclosed, open-air patio lined with giant tropical plants. She clasped her hands together saying, "What a wonderful space. I love it! It's perfect for cocktail hour." She walked around the patio twice before returning to inspect the kitchen. Upstairs, I found three bedrooms. Dad carried our over-sized suitcases upstairs and Mom started unpacking. I glanced in the master bedroom and an empty room, finally finding mine.

"Come look at my room, Mom." My room contained a bed with a flowered bedspread, a dresser, and a desk which came stocked with a notebook, three pens, and a small Spanish-English dictionary. I loved it.

I placed Chuz on the bed, sitting up against the pillows, arranged my troll collection on top of the dresser, and stacked the few books I had brought with me on the desk. I was happy. My room was set up how I liked it, and we were a family again.

Later, Mom said to Dad, "What happened? I was all ready to do battle with the desert out at the job site. I thought they provided housing for the families out there."

"They did, but it would never work. It's too far and the Sechura Desert is desolate. I don't like it and you would hate it, all drifting sand dunes and cracked earth. There's no school, and you wouldn't believe the condition of the housing. It's filthy, filled with sand and everywhere are piles of cockroach carcasses tumbling out of kitchen cabinets. Every cabinet was like that. That was the last straw. The company didn't want to pay more, but I managed to negotiate an extra housing stipend."

Mom shuddered at the mention of cockroaches, even though she had been used to a stray roach or two scuttling across the floor in Lahore. "This is great. We'll be fine here, but does that mean we only get to see you on weekends?"

"No, I'll come home on Wednesday nights as well. It's not ideal, but it's the best we can do for now."

"We'll make it work. I'm just happy to be here." Mom sounded cheerful.

"There's a school right across the street and it's not too far from Club Grau, where you and Inga can swim and meet other expats. It's named after a Peruvian naval hero who was born in Piura, and you'll find his name popping up everywhere. I wish I could stay longer to help you get settled, but Conrad, my boss, is turning out to be hard to work with. He seems to have taken an instant dislike to me and questions everything I say."

"That's too bad. Don't worry about us. I'll get to work on the school first thing. And Inga and I will love the pool, I know it."

Unfortunately, Dad had to leave the next morning for the San Lorenzo Drainage Project job site. He had already taken off a few days to travel down to Lima to meet us, then had the extra day of delay because of the arrival mix-up.

As soon as he left, Mom started slinging pots and pans in the kitchen, boiling huge vats of drinking water for us to consume. Mom remembered her experience with servants in Lahore and decided to forgo live-in help, instead hiring day staff. The cumbersome job of boiling water would last until she could hire a maid. Dad had impressed upon me the importance of never drinking tap water.

"It can make you sick, so, like in Pakistan, you can only drink water that we've boiled. We've been spoiled by living in the States for the last two years and being able to drink tap water. And no salads, milk, ice cream, or fruit that hasn't been peeled. It's all dangerous." I didn't care about salads or milk, but I'd miss ice cream. Mom made banana milkshakes with vile tasting powdered milk and boiled water so I could get enough calcium. I plugged my nose, gulped one down every day and never drank banana milkshakes for pleasure ever again once we left Peru.

BOOKS

When our shipment finally arrived from the States, I was terribly excited about the refrigerator. Mom probably was, too, so she could store more food. For me, it was what was inside. I was a voracious reader and in

San Francisco, Mom had spent weeks scouring every used bookstore she could find to buy dog-eared paperback books for me, which she stuffed inside the refrigerator.

"Mom, can I read one book before we go? Just one?" I had asked over and over before we left.

"No, keep your hands off those books. We can go to the library here, but there won't be any library with English-language books in Peru," she had said.

When we opened the refrigerator door, all the books tumbled out. I jumped up and down, grabbing as many as I could. I wanted to gather them in my arms and read them all at once. Mom packed them in a box that was kept in her closet in the master bedroom. I was rationed one book per week to make the supply last over the two years of Dad's contract. "Book day" was the highlight of my week, and I perused the books for a long time before making my selection, touching each binding, reading the titles and back covers, fanning the pages, feeling the weight of every book. Finally, I would make my decision. Usually, I wanted one that was long enough that it would last a few days, but more often I'd read it through within a day or two. After a few months, I had a nice library built up and I could pick favorites to reread. Mom found nearly complete sets of some of my favorite series with teen detectives. The books were numbered on the spine, so it was easy to read them in order, even if I didn't have all of them. Frank and Joe of the Hardy Boys caught my attention first. When I discovered Nancy Drew, I was thrilled to see that a girl could solve mysteries as well as the boys. Cherry Ames took things even further by being a nurse who solved crimes.

In the back of the house was a set of rough concrete stairs that led to a small apartment meant for servants' quarters. It was not occupied, and my parents never went there. These were my hidden stairs like the ones in *The Hidden Staircase* in the Nancy Drew series. I walked around the patio with the phantom Little Boy and Little Girl trailing along, pretending we didn't know about the stairs. Approaching them, I said, "Well, what have we here? We'd better investigate. Maybe there's a ghost at the top." We crept up the stairs, pausing before rounding the corner to make sure we weren't seen by anyone. I flattened my body against the wall and stepped softly so we didn't betray our presence. My heart pounded; my hands were damp with sweat. I looked back at Little Boy, and he nodded for me to keep going. I placed my hand softly on the door handle, grasped it firmly, and flung open the door, ready for anything. But nobody was there and there was no ghost. It still felt spooky, though.

We peeked over the wall to spy on the neighborhood behind us and watched kids kicking a soccer ball in the street and a mother bringing groceries from the market. Nothing too mysterious. We sat on the cold concrete floor in the apartment, and I pulled a small troll out of my pocket. While running my hand over its pink hair, I suddenly thought about our journey on the ship. I became enraged and threw the troll as hard as I could across the room. I grabbed it and threw it again and again. As suddenly as my rage came on, it dissipated and I sat quietly, unsure of what had just happened. One minute I was Nancy Drew, the next I was an angry little girl. What was happening to me? Little Boy and Little Girl sat with me during the outburst, quiet but comforting. After I calmed down, I went to my bedroom and picked up *The Hidden Staircase*, ready to reread the mystery and escape into a world where everything always worked out for Nancy Drew.

SCHOOL—SANTA MARIA

As soon as we were settled in our new home, Mom had to decide where I was going to school. She faced a dilemma since Piura had no American or international schools. Any of those options would have been available in Lima, a much bigger city. There were five American families in town, and only two with children—hardly enough to support an American school.

Of the two main Spanish-language schools in Piura, the one that would have made sense to attend was across the street from our house. The snooty kids next door attended the Colegio Santa Maria across town, and when their mother told Mom it was a better school, she made up her mind. My first day, I was crammed into a station wagon with a driver and the six neighbor kids who barely tolerated me. Worse, every day included Catholic church services on knees bloodied from the rough concrete. We weren't Catholic and I couldn't make sense of the long, unfamiliar masses in Spanish.

Every time I left home, Mom reminded me not to drink any tap water and gave me a bottle of boiled water. "And don't drink any milk. It's not pasteurized. You'll get your banana milkshake when you get home." The thought of the loathsome milkshakes made me grimace.

Since it was a Spanish-speaking school, Mom expected the immersion technique to be a quick way for me to learn the language. I picked up a lot of vocabulary, but was completely lost in grammar, reading, and math for most of the first few months. Urdu words from our time in Pakistan flew into my head whenever I was stuck. Writing assignments felt impossible and I couldn't decipher the gibberish that came out of the teacher's mouths. Long division was upside down and backwards—it made no sense.

A highlight of the day was recess, when I could go over to the chain-link fence that separated the girls' and boys' schools and see my friends. Morgan, who was my age, was blond and stocky, and his little brother, Gary, was blond and skinny. They were sons of one of Dad's co-workers and our parents socialized often, while we played tag and climbed trees.

I was desperate to fit in any way I could in a sea of identical light blue uniforms over white, collared, short-sleeved blouses I disliked. Every day when we returned from lunch, the six neighbor kids would burst out of the van and make a beeline to the *bole* stand. I remembered Mom's instructions, so I held back at first. I knew it was dangerous to eat ice made from unpurified water, but it was so tempting. And they didn't get sick, even though they ate them every day. They made fun of me and licked their frozen treats slowly to taunt me. It didn't take long for me to break down. The first bite flooded my mouth with a delicious mixture of sweet, tart, and cold. It was a scorching day and tiny beads of sugary melt were already forming. I quickly licked it with my tongue like a cat lapping milk. That made it melt faster, so I took another bite, the icy sweetness sliding coolly down my throat. In a few bites, it was gone and nothing bad happened. I didn't get sick. What a relief. I was fine, no danger.

BULLETS

One day, I was sitting at my desk at school, trying to make sense of a word problem, muddling through the text with my well-worn Spanish-English dictionary. I hoped I had the gist of it and then set to work on the puzzling long-division. Suddenly I heard the unmistakable rat-tat-tat of gunfire from a machine gun. I automatically slid to the floor under my desk. The war-time memory of Lahore stirred as I took cover. There was mass pandemonium as the other kids jumped out of their seats and ran to the windows, while teachers ran back and forth to other classrooms. There was no more gunfire after the initial burst. It was announced eventually that school was canceled for the day and cars clogged the entrance as worried parents arrived to collect their children. The bossy eldest child from next door rounded up me and all her siblings, trying to get her arms around all of us, for once including me in the brood. This time, I was thankful for her can-do attitude. We were driven to their house, where their mother gave us cookies and kept us safely inside.

Later, Mom arrived, frantic, after hearing the bullets while running errands, squeezing me tightly when I ran toward her. As we walked toward our front gate, we could see a small hole in the concrete next to our front door. "A bullet hole!" she said.

"Woooooow," I said, drawing the word out, shocked that a bullet found our house. I poked my finger into the hole. The rough concrete felt gritty. We walked around to the side yard. "Look, there's another one," I said, finding a bullet in the dirt.

"We'd better get inside in case there are more shots." We found two more bullet holes in Mom's and Dad's room. "I wish Dad was home," said Mom.

Seeing the four bullet holes made it all too real. Mom kept us near the center of the house, away from windows in case more bullets came. Were we at war again? We didn't have any information about what was going on. I tried to read a Nancy Drew book in my room with Little Boy and Little Girl, but I kept thinking about the bullets. Could Nancy Drew solve the case of the sprayed bullets? She'd probably want to interview some people, such as the mayor or the chief of police, and then investigate the area where the bullets originated. I told Little Boy and Little Girl that we should start by drawing up a list of people we could interview, including eyewitnesses. We were working on our list when I heard the front door open, and Dad call out.

Dad had been at the San Lorenzo project but drove back as soon as he heard the news. A soldier at the Air Force base, next to the municipal airport, had been cleaning a mounted machine gun and accidentally hit something that triggered the spray of bullets. The house next door took thirty bullets. In another house, a man was eating breakfast, holding his newspaper up when a bullet tore through the paper.

We were so relieved we weren't at war—it was only an accident.

It wasn't until Dad went upstairs to unpack that he found that the bullet that shattered the window had traveled through the closet, leaving a bullet hole in every one of his collared shirts and coats. He dug the bullet out of the wall and held it up for us to see. The copper-colored bullet was over two inches long and heavier than I expected. I held it in my hand, imagining the horror of what it could have done if it had hit me. Mom shuddered and said, "I hate to think . . . " without finishing her sentence.

That night, Dad walked around the house securing all the windows and doors, as he usually did, but with extra fervor, as if he could control random bullets flying through the air by assuring that the windows were closed.

Peru was turning out to have a lot of ordeals, and I wasn't sure I liked it very much.

6

Exploring Peru

FRIENDS

One weekend day, I shouted, "Mom, I'm going out."

"I thought you were climbing the tree out front," Mom said from upstairs.

"I was. Now I'm going to ride my bike to the store."

"OK, be careful," she said, and with those words, delicious freedom was mine. When Santa brought me a used blue bike, slightly dented, for Christmas, my range quadrupled, and I didn't need to be driven everywhere.

Pedaling down the sun-dappled street to the small *tienda* a couple of blocks away, my allowance in soles jingled in my pocket with every pump of my legs. I examined the limited collection of candy and soft drinks under the single glass counter in the tiny, open storefront, finally settling on two of my favorites, Fanta and Chicklets gum. I sat on the curb as I guzzled the ice-cold orange drink and plotted my route back home, keeping a sharp eye out for anything unusual in case I could collect evidence to solve mysteries like Nancy Drew.

I rode through the shabby neighborhood with untidy yards full of kids and toys. It was a world away from our quiet, well-tended street one block over. Pedaling toward a noisy group kicking a soccer ball in the street, I stopped short when the ball tumbled toward me. I gave it a tentative kick and they laughed and gestured for me to join them. I was nervous because my Spanish was rudimentary, but I got through the basics and stuttered out my name.

Returning home later, I burst through the door. "Mom, I made some new friends."

"You did? Where?" she asked, sounding doubtful. When I described who they were and where I met them, she seemed pleased. "That's wonderful. Maybe next time you could invite them over." I wasn't too sure about that. What would we do or talk about? I couldn't see pulling that off.

The next weekend, I skipped tree climbing and took my bike on the same route. The kids waved and kicked the ball to me, but I got tongue tied when one of the mothers came out of her house, wiping her hands on her apron, asking me questions in rapid-fire Spanish. I told her my name and after a couple of repetitions, I picked up "comida" and "ahora." Was she inviting me to dinner? Miraculously, I understood an entire sentence when she asked where my mother was: "Donde esta tu madre?" I pointed to the back of our house. She took my hand, and we walked to the house, my bike wobbling in my other hand. With translation help from our maid, Mom agreed to not only dinner, but an overnight visit. She thought it was a great idea, making cross-cultural connections and all that. I was nervous about the overnight part, but the ball was rolling so fast I couldn't control it, and, in a flash, Mom had packed a little overnight bag and off I went.

I was stiff and awkward at first but loosened up in the company of the boisterous family chatter, so different from our quiet family, despite not understanding most of what they said. We ate a simple but delicious dinner of chicken and rice and played a coin-tossing game. I couldn't follow all of it, but they didn't care, and we all laughed a lot. When it was bedtime, their mother shepherded us through tooth brushing and all three of the kids piled onto the double bed. I stood awkwardly by the bed, not sure what to do, but they made room for me, and I crawled in on the side. I had never slept with anyone except my mother, and I tried to stay very still so I wouldn't wake anyone. Their soft, regular breathing told me they were asleep instantly, but I was wide eyed for a long time, absorbing all the new sights and sounds of the evening.

In the morning, fried eggs with a slightly runny yolk and delicate crispy edges around the egg white, served on warmed leftover rice, was a highlight for me. It was so different from my usual cereal. After I told Mom about it, she started making it for me and it became one of my favorite breakfasts.

The next week, I was excited to tell the next-door neighbor kids about my new friends, thinking I'd gain some credibility. However, the bossy oldest girl grilled me about where my new friends lived. When I described the location, she tilted her nose up and said, "No good. Bad people." Evidently, she deemed the densely built houses behind us as being lower class and had no interest in hearing more. I remained friendly with my new pals but understood there was a divide between the two groups of Peruvians that I would have to straddle.

SCHOOL-CALVERT

My next school was an experiment. Mom could tell I wasn't happy, and my poor grades reflected my lack of progress at Santa Maria. The bullet incident had left us all shaken and even though it had nothing to do with the school, it precipitated a change.

One day, when I was dodging a rowdy group of blond, fair-skinned American kids dunking each other in the pool at Club Grau, I noticed Mom talking animatedly with a woman at the restaurant where all the expat adults socialized. The woman turned out to be the mother of the unruly group of siblings in the pool. On the way home, Mom told me all about Mrs. Hancock and the kids.

"The Hancock's are missionaries and Joyce, their mother, has been teaching her kids at home for the past two years using the Calvert Correspondence School," said Mom. "Mr. Hancock is busy with the mission work, which Joyce also helps with."

Does that mean he's at home every night?

No, he travels like Daddy, but instead of going to a single job site, he goes all over preaching the word of God.

"What is Calvert? Do they read books on their own? How do they learn anything?"

"The materials are sent from Baltimore; their mom goes through it with them, and assignments are sent back to a teacher in the States.

"No tests?" I liked the sound of that.

"Yes, silly, there are tests. They get sent to the States. Their mother invited you to join them because if they had one more kid in their 'school,' their mission will send a teacher from the States." Anything in English sounded good to me, and no more Catholic mass or uniforms sounded even better. I liked the kids in the family, especially David, who was my age and very funny.

One day, a big cardboard box arrived in the mail. Mom slit the top with a knife to expose a treasure trove of brand-new books with glossy covers that were smooth to the touch. They even smelled new. There were textbooks for every subject, teacher's guides for the two moms, notebooks, pens, and pencils. I was in heaven. I liked office supplies almost as much as books. I grabbed the books that interested me the most, including all the ones that had pure reading, such as English literature, history, and geography. I took my hoard up to my room and started in, consuming all the literature and my first poetry book, *This Singing World Junior Edition*, before we even started classes.

When I walked into the spare rooftop room at the Hancock's, I was amazed. It had been transformed into a proper schoolroom with a large white board hanging on the brick wall and sturdy wooden desks for each of us. Mom and Mrs. Hancock took turns with the day-to-day instruction and oversaw our tests and essays, which were mailed to Baltimore. I loved getting letters from my teacher, who was always supportive and encouraging ... a lot more encouraging than Mom, who got impatient with me.

Once the new mission teacher arrived, I thrived in the Calvert program, voraciously reading books, writing essays, studying, and learning everything I could. It was as if a dam opened in me and the whole world flooded in. Geology, European art history, the Nile River, King Tutankhamen, and the Egyptian pyramids all became vivid and real to me. My grades shot up, and I looked forward to school every day. Even math wasn't that bad, and we did long division the normal way.

OUCH

Things were looking up, but my struggles with Peru weren't over. From the beginning in Peru, my body felt different, and I was stuck in a perpetual cycle of injuries and illnesses. As soon as I'd recover from one, another calamity would befall me.

In the afternoons, I loved to climb the big, leafy tree in front of our house. We had a small garden with a low fence and on the other side of the sidewalk was the tree. I could climb up the trunk, slide my foot in a saddle between a sturdy branch and the trunk, and launch myself into the air with my arms outstretched to grab a horizontal branch like a gymnast on parallel bars. I'd swing back and forth, drop to the ground, and go up again. A tall, slim police officer in a sharp uniform paced up and down the sidewalk across the street, guarding a government building. I waved to him, and he waved back. One day, I launched off the tree, missed the branch, fell to the ground, and hit my head. It was lights out for me. That's all I remember.

Later, Mom told me she opened the door after a knock to find the police officer holding my limp body, my head hanging over one arm and legs dangling over the other. She thought I was dead.

I lay unconscious in a hospital bed for three days. No tests were conducted because they had no equipment. Rest was the best treatment for a concussion and my body enforced this by knocking me out. The doctors didn't want to move me, thinking that movement might make things worse. After the third day, I woke up wondering where I was and why Mom and Dad looked so worried. I was discharged as soon as I woke up, barely registering anything about the hospital other than a hazy memory of white walls and an antiseptic odor. Mom made me rest far more days than I wanted to, even though I kept telling her I felt fine. So far, I had dodged bullets and a head injury, but the cycle continued.

My secret pleasure of the frozen *boles* was still safe, and I continued enjoying my treat every day at school without Mom finding out that I was breaking the rules. Late one night, it all came crashing down. Damp with sweat, my sheets entangled with my body, my bed suddenly too small, I rolled and writhed. "Daddy, my stomach hurts." Dad leaned over me, looking serious. Mom hovered behind him. I cried out when he pressed gently on my abdomen. Time wobbled and a new face appeared at my bedside. A doctor examined me and spoke quietly but urgently to my parents.

The next thing I knew, I was in a room at the Catholic hospital, wracked with fever and pierced with sharp abdominal pains. The cool sheets were white and crisp when I slid between them, the iron bedstead surrounded by pale blue walls. I faded in and out of a feverish delirium, the sheets becoming hot as a furnace. The old nightmare of Mom and me being separated on the train tracks in Tokyo plagued me, but every time I opened my eyes, Mom was there, wiping a damp washcloth across my forehead. In my recurring nightmare, the doors always slam shut before Mom can reach me.

The clutching abdominal pain scared the doctor into doing an appendectomy, thinking my appendix was inflamed. Despite the surgery, the drenching fevers continued and now I had a three-inch slice in my lower right abdomen in addition to the cramping abdominal pain. Dad, who missed nothing, wondered what was up with the massive doses of antibiotics being pumped through my IV. Upon being questioned, the doctor announced that I had typhoid fever, not appendicitis. My parents were in shock.

"How could this be with all the care we've taken to purify our drinking water and clean the produce we eat? How is this possible?" Mom asked. There was more questioning, now directed at me. In my weakened condition, I broke down and told them about the *boles*. Dad sighed and Mom went quiet and pale, but they didn't scold me for eating the icy treat contaminated with the bacteria that causes typhoid. They were more worried about whether I would live or die.

The first day after surgery, I couldn't even straighten up because of the pain from the incision, but each day I grew stronger. After many days, the steps became less labored, and I could shuffle outside to the tiled courtyard between the hospital and the chapel in my oversized, fluffy slippers and quilted robe, my brown hair plaited into two thick braids. The antibiotics worked their magic and slowly the fevers abated.

Nurses breezed in and out of my hospital room and one of my parents was there around the clock. Dad read to me from *The Swiss Family Robinson* in his steady baritone, keeping the red, hardcover book on the bed stand when he wasn't around. I liked escaping to a remote island in New Guinea as much as getting outside, away from my hospital room. Mom took me on walks every day. It was painful to even take a step, but I looked forward to being outside where I could feel the warmth of the shimmering sun on my cheeks every day, elated that the heat was coming from outside my body instead of inside.

"Can you go a few more steps on your big day?" Mom had been coaxing me a little further each day, inching toward the arched doorway with the heavy, carved door that led to the hospital chapel on the other side of the sunny courtyard. This was our goal, to get all the way across the courtyard and back to the ward by my birthday. On the 15th day of December, on my tenth birthday, we finally made it. In this arid, equatorial land of the Sechura Desert, seasons didn't mean much, and the temperature was over ninety degrees Fahrenheit. The effort of walking left me damp with sweat, only this time it was from exertion and not fevers. I happily returned to my room to slide between the cool sheets, grateful for my returning strength and a slice of birthday cake.

My string of bad luck wasn't over, though. Once I was out of the hospital, the incision healed fully, and Mom and I went back to battling over banana milkshakes. I was coaxed out of the house by an invitation to swim at Club Grau. The Hancock's were going, and I liked reconnecting with my classmates from our tiny one-room school.

Their dad was in a jovial mood, spending hours with us in the water. His kids delighted in diving off his shoulders, gliding smoothly into the clear water. I kept turning down his offer to dive, but he kept encouraging me. When I finally agreed, I imitated what I thought his kids were doing and dove off his shoulders. I dropped like a rock. Then sudden contact. A shuddering stop. Pain. Sharp pain. Throbbing pain. Where was it coming from? My head felt like it was exploding. I came up shrieking, arms flailing. I didn't know what happened, and neither did anyone else, because I was windmilling around in the water. The missionary dad grabbed me and felt all over my head, then got a look at my mouth. He gaped, wiping the water from his eyes as if he couldn't believe what he saw. Missing were most of my two front teeth. They were at the bottom of the pool, smashed into a thousand pieces like grains of calcified sand.

I was brought home and, again, Mom was confronted by a man carrying me in his arms. Mrs. Hancock told Mom she felt terrible and wished it had been one of her own kids. Dental care in Piura was rudimentary, and I had become used to having cavities filled without a local anesthetic, gripping the armrests with white-knuckled fingers. When the drilling hit a nerve, I felt like I was falling, falling, falling into a black hole. The dentist put something on my front tooth nubs to protect them from air hitting the nerve and sent us to Lima by plane. Luckily, the nubs were large enough that caps could be attached. They were larger than my original teeth, so I felt like Bugs Bunny, but at least they covered the nerve and took the pain away. Mom put on a brave face, but I could tell she was distraught.

Not long after that, a pimple appeared on my chin. So minor, so normal, but it grew and grew until it was the size of a watermelon to me. *What now?* When Mom announced a doctor's visit, I wanted to cry. *No more doctors!* There was minimal pain, but after two hospital stays and a dental emergency, the thought of seeing another doctor felt monumental.

"More hospitals?" I asked.

"No, don't be so dramatic. It's just a little thing." Mom pooh-poohed my fears, but I was filled with dread. They diagnosed a staph infection, lanced it, and placed a bulky white bandage over the drain. When I saw the bandage, which was the size of a house, I wanted to stay in the hospital rather than walk around with that on my face, humiliated. When we got back from the clinic, I couldn't stop crying.

"What's wrong? Does it hurt that much?" asked Mom.

"No, but how long will I be like this? First my teeth and now this. I can't go out with this bandage on my face. I've already missed so much school."

"I know, but you can study at home. This won't be as bad as being in the hospital. I promise."

I checked at least sixteen times a day, but the bandage was still hideous. I hid in my room with Little Boy and Little Girl, escaping into my book. I bolted back to Dal Lake, the wondrous place where I caught my first fish in Kashmir, in Rumer Godden's book, *Kingfishers Catch Fire*. She transported me there with her words, taking me with her as she traveled with Sophie and her two children. I relived a happy time in my life, before all these mishaps befell me.

HUACOS

A sharp knock on the door startled us one evening, visitors being rare. The bandages had come off my face by then, I was getting used to my new teeth, and I was less shy of people seeing me. Dad opened the door to a small, Peruvian man with sepia skin, few teeth, and a face full of wrinkles; over his shoulder, he carried a large sack. They exchanged a few words in Spanish as he entered, setting his dirty cloth bag down with exquisite gentleness on the black-and-white tiles in our living room. Sitting cross-legged on the floor, he drew out his treasures, placing fragile pottery full of muddy earth tones—brown, tan, yellow, burnt orange and reddish hues—on a low table. Out of his mouth flowed words in Spanish, another dialect, perhaps Quechua, and English, but one word stood out: *huaco*. As the man murmured softly, Dad shared what he knew about *huacos*, an ancient form of pottery created by the earliest inhabitants of Peru, long before the Incas. He picked one up with rough-cut lines decorating the top and said the low-slung bowl might have been made by the first people who lived here, maybe around the time the pyramids were being built in Egypt; he remembered I was learning about pyramids in school.

The man pointed at the smallest ceramic and then pointed at me. "I think he's saying these small ones were made for children," Mom said.

He held his hand out, palm up, fingers curled slightly. I held my hand to match his. A diminutive *huaco,* brick red with geometric grooves around the spout, was placed tenderly in my palm with one hand, while the other hand cupped my fingers around it securely. I couldn't imagine that I was holding something so old. Cool in my hand, the smooth, rounded bottom of the earthen pot, marked with blackened streaks, evoked a vision of a woman shaping a slab of wet clay into a sphere. Two thousand years later, I was holding the sculpted bowl in my hand. Energy buzzed through me like a charged current carrying messages from a scribe from the past.

"Do you want to pick one out?" Mom asked. Cradled in the palm of my hand, the miniature pot fit perfectly, like it was made for me.

"I'll choose this one," I said.

My miniature collection grew alongside the larges pieces that Mom and Dad acquired from the *huaqueros,* the men who traveled across the desert to share their treasures with us, but my first was forever my favorite.

"Dad, why did that man have such dark skin? Most of the Peruvians look like us, or at least they look like me when I have a tan."

"Most of the Peruvians we know descended from the Spanish conquerors. That man with the *huacos* came from the original Peruvians. You remember when you learned about the Native Americans in the Southwest of the US? It's like that. There were native South Americans, too," he said.

"You mean like the people who made your arrowheads?" I asked.

"Yes, I collected some of those arrowheads in Kansas, but mostly in Colorado, near Colorado State, where I went to school. The Native American men used tools to shape all the different designs from rocks. Each design had a different purpose. The Native American women made beautiful, tightly woven baskets with intricate designs. Some colors and designs on the *huacos* remind me of the designs on those baskets. It's possible the women created the *haucos* here, too. The *huacos* are special and show us how skilled they were in shaping, firing, and decorating the clay."

"Was mine a toy? It's so small."

"I don't know for sure. It could have been a toy, or it might have been used as part of their funeral rituals when someone died."

I looked at my *huaco*, wondering who made the small object and for what purpose. Was it a woman, whose child watched her shape the clay? Or was it a woman who had lost her child to sickness or an accident?

HIDDEN TREASURES

Despite my challenges, we had some enjoyable times in Peru. Mom was flourishing, making friends, learning about the local culture, and sipping Pisco Sours. She socialized with all five of the American families, especially Lori Pike, Morgan's mother, and made several Peruvian friends who introduced her to wonderful local foods. We all grew to love ceviche and fried calamari rings—especially the tentacles—and seafood stews with fresh fish caught off the coast.

We'd go to Morgan's house and while the adults were enjoying their cocktails, Morgan, Gary, and I would run off to play with our miniature metal Corgi cars and trucks in the shady front yard where we could race our cars on the paved path. Their big grassy backyard was bordered by a low stone fence, but we liked to go beyond the fence into the desert to explore natural stone outcroppings that we weren't supposed to touch because they could harbor scorpions or rattlesnakes. We poked our fingers into the crevices of the rocks, sometimes remembering to use a stick first to scare off any creatures. We had to see if there were any hidden treasures in there, but there never was unless it was a Corgi car we had left.

When our fathers had time off work, we'd take weekend trips with the Pike family. Little rustic cabins at the beach an hour from Piura was a favorite destination. Long barrel waves rolled in gently on a sweep of beach where, at regular intervals, a three-sided fence structure was set up for swimming to protect against stingrays. I was always relieved to escape without a sting, having had enough of doctors, hospitals, and altered body parts. While my skin wrinkled after being in the salt water so long, it also tanned quickly to a deep bronze, thanks to inheriting Dad's olive complexion.

After a long stretch of too much routine and not enough excursions, Mom said, "Carroll, let's take a trip out to the project site. I want to see it for myself, to see if it's as bleak as you say. Lori wants to go, too. I'm so happy to have friends who want to explore. How bad could it be?" Mom busied herself with the plans.

"Oh, it's bad. I see what you mean," she said when we arrived with the Pikes after dodging sand dunes drifting across the rough road, threatening to hide it like invisible ink. "It's . . . austere. There's not a tree in sight."

Morgan and I, however, were captivated by the vast expanse of cracked hardpan as far as the eye could see, spreading like a giant nebula, and saw the potential for creating our own irrigation systems. The adults went off for a tour of the San Lorenzo Project, a World Bank-funded irrigation scheme to increase crops and encourage population growth in this area of the Chira-Piura Region of Peru. Dad and Mr. Pike were working on a feasibility study to increase water distribution systems and the eventual construction of a dam for their employer, IECo.

While the adults were busy, Morgan and Gary and I quickly set to work behind the house where Dad stayed, armed with a pitcher of water. We used a stick to expand the width of the natural cracks and plugged channels to direct the water where we wanted it, creating an elaborate system to move water around.

As we drove home, Mom said, "You seemed to have fun out there. Maybe you'd like to stay out there with Dad?" What? There was no town and no schools or stores. I gave her a sharp look but saw her teasing grin.

"I think Piura is fine," I said. "It helps to know where he is when he's not home, and now I can understand why we can't live there with him. But I wish he could be with us in Piura."

"Me too," she said. "Me too."

MACHU PICCHU

Machu Picchu was better than I had hoped, once I finally got there. The plane angled up so high I thought we would fall back to earth. Higher and higher we went, darting through narrow notches in the jagged peaks of the Andes. When I thought we could go no higher, a shallow, green bowl drew us in, and we landed with a thud and a bounce on the paved airstrip in Cusco.

On the train ride from Cusco to Machu Picchu, I was glued to the window while Mom read aloud from a guidebook as we chugged up to the arch of Tica Tica, then rolled downhill toward Machu Picchu at 8,000 feet. Mom talked about Inca advances in astronomy and how they appeased their gods through child sacrifice. I shivered when I heard that. How brutal.

I was invigorated by Machu Picchu. Set on an improbable terraced mountaintop, surrounded by tall angular peaks and bottomless valleys, it was hidden from sight until we were practically upon it. Few other tourists were around, and we could roam freely throughout the ruins.

My pleated plaid dress slapped against my thighs as I ran through the grassy terraces of Machu Picchu. Below the lowest terrace, the ground dropped steeply into a frothing river, a silvery ribbon that sliced through the thick, green jungle joining this heavenly world to middle earth. Panting, I sat on great blocks of smooth fossil-gray stone and gazed at the Temple of the Sun, where people, perhaps girls my age, were sacrificed.

I wondered if a girl like me sat here 500 years ago, worshipping the sun.

ABRUPT END

In October 1968, a military coup resulted in a new Peruvian president, Juan Velasco Alvarado. Since that time, there had been increasing activity from a new communist guerilla group agitating for change and there was concern about violence. Dad said military coups happened so often in South America that it would have been unusual if we didn't experience one. However, Mom and Dad were a little gun-shy of rebellions and didn't want to take a chance on another military evacuation.

* * *

I was starting sixth grade and things were changing, but I couldn't figure out why. I wanted to talk with David about more serious things than our usual goofing around, but suddenly felt awkward. It was the same with Morgan, but his little brother, Gary, was always hanging around wanting to play. I didn't know what I wanted to talk about, but I had feelings I wanted to understand, and I was more conscious of my body. The boys didn't respond to my mumbling attempts to talk about deeper subjects, so I left our visits feeling flustered and unsettled.

"We're going home," Dad said one day. I didn't understand what he meant because we were home. Our home was in Piura.

"We're going home to the States," he elaborated. That was baffling. Maybe it was home to them, but for me, I had lived longer in other countries than in the US. It was home to them, but I felt more comfortable just about anywhere other than the States—put me in an airport, or on an airplane, or anywhere with other kids who moved around, and I felt at home. I wished we were going directly to another country, instead of always having to go back to the States.

"What about your project? Is it finished?"

"The feasibility study is just about done and it's up to the Peruvian government to decide if they want to move to the next phase. The results are promising, so I think the project will continue. If so, IECo will have to bid on it, just like before."

Once my parents decided to leave on their own terms, a few months before the contract ended, we sped through the last two months of sixth-grade schoolwork and mailed my tests and essays to my teacher. We boxed up my beloved books and left them with another family. Dad packed the silver in the Pan Am bag—this time he could carry it.

The last few times I saw David at school and Morgan at his house when we visited, I wanted to say more about how much I would miss them and how much their friendship meant to me, but I didn't have the right words. I kept putting it off until we were all standing at the airport, and time ran out like sand slipping through my fingers.

The whole American contingent turned out at the airport with the Hancock's, our teacher, the Pikes with Morgan and Gary, some Peruvian friends, and all my dad's co-workers. We boarded the plane, and I waved back at everyone, feeling vaguely dissatisfied that I had left something behind —my unspoken words.

7

San Francisco
City Life

SAN FRANCISCO

Back in the States, I started sixth grade amidst a changing body. I tried to staunch the dribble of blood between my legs with toilet paper until Mom accidentally walked in on me in the bathroom, as shocked as I was that my period started. She had told me all about it but neither of us expected it this early. I was only eleven. The bulky pads she got me worked better than toilet paper, but I was bitter that I couldn't go swimming. My favorite play clothes didn't look right over my developing breast buds and my highwater pants didn't look cool with my ankles sticking out. My legs ached with a growth spurt, and I shot up to five feet six inches. I wanted to go back to my old body.

I hoped I could go back to Lafayette Elementary School, but that didn't happen. Mom quickly found us a house, but it was in the Sunset District, far on the opposite side of Golden Gate Park from where we lived before, meaning I would attend Ulloa Elementary School. It was mostly a social experience since I had already finished the school year in Peru. I sailed through testing for grade placement and played the name game efficiently with my teacher on the first day of class, explaining right away that I went by my middle name, and I pronounced my last name slowly for her. Adept at playing Four Square and Wall Ball, I made friends easily.

I used the time wisely by acquiring my first boyfriend. It meant little to me, other than giving me social standing. This relationship was notable for being the first but was otherwise underwhelming. The affair consisted of a note from a popular boy asking if I would be his girlfriend, which gave me a boost of credibility with my peers. After consulting with a twittering quiver of girls, I passed a "yes" note through an intermediary. He and I sat together at lunch one day, but when he drifted away, I gathered that the fling was over. What did I do wrong? I didn't understand the rules of this new game.

During the summer, I fell in love, but not with a boy. Ice skating stole my heart, allowing my new gangly body on my tall frame to become graceful, floating across the ice effortlessly. Mom took me to a rink near Ocean Beach, close to our house, where I took my first wobbly steps onto the novelty of frozen water. Dropped off early Saturday mornings for group lessons, followed by hours of free skating and on Tuesday evenings for private lessons, I rapidly mastered Alpha, Beta, and Gamma levels, with patches to prove it. Mom perfected the art of sewing skating dresses with short, frilly skirts, and I found my first sports passion.

My first trip to a US dentist after Peru was a revelation. A cavity needed to be filled, but I refused Novocain, fearing the needle, and preferring the Peruvian way, without anesthetic. A verbal tussle ensued, but finally the dentist agreed. I clutched the arms of the dental chair until my knuckles turned white, squeezed my eyes shut, and prepared for the ordeal. The dentist set the drill down after a few minutes, but I knew it hadn't been long enough. After a long pause, he said, "I can't do this. It's child abuse," and went to get my mother. He returned with a proposal.

"You're very brave, the bravest girl I know, but it doesn't need to be this way. How about if you let me numb your mouth once and see if you aren't more comfortable? After all, I tried it your way and I can see that you're in pain. The shot hurts for a second, but then you won't feel anything." I agreed, cried when the needle went in, and instantly regretted my decision. Never again, I thought. My hands gripped the arms of the chair when the drilling started but, to my amazement, there was no pain, just a deep vibration and the familiar sound of the drill. I finally saw what he meant. Going to the dentist didn't need to hurt, and I didn't need to be that brave.

During the time in San Francisco, Dad was a remote Project Manager for a study of asphalt canal linings for the government of Mexico and I wondered if we'd move there next. At least I knew Spanish. Mom picked up friendships she had made the last time we lived in San Francisco and pestered Dad about when we'd move again. "When a position opens up, that's when we'll move," was his response. She was more than ready whenever or wherever. For her, anywhere was better than an ordinary life in the States.

PRESIDIO JUNIOR HIGH SCHOOL

Over the summer, we moved to the Richmond District on 29th Avenue, a half block from Golden Gate Park, and three blocks from my new school, Presidio Junior High. It was exactly halfway between Lafayette and Alamo Elementary Schools, my two elementary schools, so I was back in my old neighborhood. I didn't remember anyone, though. The school stretched over a city block, with an imposing three-story building and asphalt play areas. I had to adjust to racing to classrooms every period but fancied learning to play the flute in music class. I loved the shiny silver instrument, so cool against my fingers, and learned to jiggle the key under my fourth finger that always stuck. I strutted around, carrying the compact black leather carrying case like a purse. The crystal clear, pure tones delighted me, even though I appeared to be tone deaf. Being part of the school orchestra made me feel like I belonged, attached to a group where I had a role to play.

Gloria, a girl who looked like me, with similar facial features, height, and long brown hair, befriended me. I went to her house often, skittering past her stern Hungarian mother. Gloria knew all about makeup, music, and boys and was the perfect guide to urban pre-teen culture. She tried to protect me from some school bullies who kept threatening to beat me up if I didn't stay away from their boyfriends . . . whoever they were.

Burying myself in *Harriet the Spy*, a novel about a young girl my age who had a regular spy route in her neighborhood, I tried to emulate her routine. Harriet scribbled notes in a composition book about everything she saw. I had the perfect spy setup in my room, which looked out to our backyard, and beyond that to the back of an apartment building. Every evening, the building façade looked like a stack of television screens as I watched one window after another light up when the occupants arrived home. I noted who came home first, who had a regular schedule, who undressed without pulling the shades and who watched the most TV. It was a great distraction from my fears about the bullies and not fitting in.

PIANO

Mom dragged me to piano lessons, which I secretly liked, but hated it when she nagged me every day to practice. We had a player piano at home that she got second or third hand at a garage sale.

"I don't even have to learn how to play. The piano plays itself." I thought this was a clever ploy, but it turned out to be ineffective.

"That's not the point. Go practice for half an hour before dinner."

My teacher, Mrs. Schmidt, was bland and pleasant, with an air of tension that reflected hours of coaxing slim strands of talent from clumsy fingers.

"I have a surprise for you," she said one day. "You've progressed so much that I would like you to take part in a recital. You may select two songs, and we'll work on those for the next few weeks until the performance."

I was proud to be chosen, Mom and Dad were thrilled, and soon the big day was upon us. I could play both songs backwards and forwards in my sleep. When it was my turn, I stepped up to the piano and played the first piece flawlessly. I was startled by a robust round of applause and, without warning, I grew self-conscious. Everything flew out of my head and away from my fingers, leaving them useless. Mrs. Schmidt motioned it was time to start the second piece. I placed my fingers on the keys, confident that the well-practiced song would flow past the dam of stage fright. There wasn't even a trickle. The room receded, and I stared at my wooden hands as though they belonged to someone else. Mrs. Schmidt came over and spoke to me in a whisper.

"What's wrong?"

"I forgot the song."

"Are you sure?"

"I'm sure. I'll just do the one song." I stood up.

"No, wait right here. I'll get the music for you."

"No, I can't." I don't know why I couldn't. It was over. The raisin was back, just like when I was on the ship in Peru, sucking my entire universe inside of it and leaving me without any memory of how to play the piano. We went back and forth, but I was adamant. I would sit on this bench until the sun went down and everyone went home if I had to. My fingers stiffened like crab's claws. I no longer knew how to play. Mom came over and took my hand.

"It's OK. One song is enough, Mrs. Schmidt. Thank you." Mom told me I didn't need to be embarrassed, and I wasn't. I felt nothing but relief that the moment was over, and I was free again, free to move and feel and not be forced into something I didn't want to do. It was as if all my energy was now able to expand.

GLORIA

Gloria was an enormous support. She listened to my travails, sympathized with me, and kept an eye out for me in the halls. When she talked with me about her boyfriend, she sounded so mature. Since we already looked somewhat alike, it wasn't hard to style myself like her, parting my long brown hair on the side like hers. I begged Mom for a pea coat like hers to protect me from the cold, foggy days. Bellbottom jeans at school were a step too far, and Mom forbade it, making me wear dresses and Mary Janes. I could never be as cool as Gloria, but I had my pea coat.

Shockingly, Gloria's boyfriend, Jay, smoked cigarettes—so grown up. All my friends in Peru had been children who played board games and hide-and-seek, while here, kids my age seemed to act like adults. Then Gloria told me he smoked marijuana. I didn't even know what that was. She confided how worried she was when he started taking pills that made him sleepy. It was a lot to take in.

One day, we were in Gloria's bedroom. "Did you notice how tense my mom was?"

"No more than usual. Are you fighting again?" I replied.

"She knows something's up with Jay."

"She's never liked him."

"Yes, but it's more than that. I have to show you something." She listened at her closed door and cracked it open a hair to see if her mother was there. "All clear." She stood in front of her mirror, and I wondered what she was going to show me. Looking into the mirror, she glanced at me, then back at the mirror, her hand on the bottom of her blouse. "OK, ready?"

"Yes, what is it?" She lifted her shirt, and her belly was enormous. She looked like a different person, her belly misshapen and blobby and all wrong. "What's wrong with your stomach? It's so big."

"I'm pregnant." The words hung in the air. I couldn't piece it all together. *Pregnant* was what adults did, not kids. She had a boyfriend, yes, but that only meant you ate lunch together and maybe kissed at China Beach when we could get away from our parents. We were only twelve.

"How? How did this happen?"

She rolled her eyes. "You know how it happened. We had sex. And now Mom's been asking me why I'm wearing baggy sweaters. I think she knows."

"She's going to kill you. What are you going to do?"

"Nothing. I can keep her off my back a little longer."

"But what then? You can't keep it a secret forever." She had no answers. Neither did I.

"Can you get married?"

Gloria blanched. "Heavens no, and Jay has problems, too. Now he's into heroin. It's too much for me." It was too much for me, as well.

Her mother glared at me when I left and that night, she called my mother and told her I couldn't visit after school anymore. She didn't know what was going on with Gloria, but she felt that she had lost control and couldn't guarantee my safety. Mom asked me about it, but I told her Gloria's mother was always mad at her and I didn't know why. I still saw Gloria at school, but we could only have hurried conversations, and I could never get anything out of her about a plan.

For the months we were in San Francisco, I felt like I was on an escalator jammed in overdrive, carrying me faster and faster into grown-up troubles. Gloria—how would her saga end? Her boyfriend—already with a heroin habit? Were those big girls who kept threatening me going to cause trouble? Little Boy and Little Girl had evaporated, incapable of dealing with issues of this magnitude.

Mom and Dad called me to the dining table one evening with an announcement. Dad was smiling and Mom looked giddy, her eyes shining like they always did when we were getting ready to go overseas. The way they never did when we were returning to the States, the place they insisted on calling home. We were moving to Dacca, East Pakistan (now Dhaka, Bangladesh). Did I know where that was? No, but I didn't care. Relief flooded through me. Yes, this was the answer, better than any solution I could dream of. Yes, I would levitate out of here, away from all these big, unsolvable problems. Yes, I welcomed the leaving, my liberation. The sooner, the better. Everyone else would have to figure it out on their own. After glancing at the map to see that East Pakistan was a hop and skip from Lahore, I ran to my room to start packing. I was going back to a place that might feel more like home to me. I was free.

8

Soft Landing in East Pakistan

DACCA

Excitement tinged with foreboding consumed me as we touched down on the tarmac in front of the squat, low slung, white-columned Dacca airport in the midst of a massive flood. Just a week before Mom and I landed in November 1970, Cyclone Bhola, the deadliest tropical cyclone ever recorded, razed much of the outlying areas with fierce winds, massive rains, and a storm surge that overwhelmed the web of waterways.

East Pakistan sparkles emerald-green, a watery province bounded by four rivers originating in the pure snows of the lofty Himalaya. Flowing through the mighty Ganges Delta, the tributaries nourish rice paddies and jute fields before filtering through the network of mangroves into the Bay of Bengal. Straddling the Tropic of Cancer, the low-lying plains are often sodden following drenching monsoons. The sights and sounds of colorful rickshaws and buses, men dressed in their long plaid *lungis* squatting by their fruit and vegetable stands, and the call to prayer were all comfortable and normal to me. A homecoming, even though it wasn't even close to Lahore. The smells of the spices, damp earth, and kerosene released a flood of nostalgic memories from our time in Lahore. With my long, lanky legs, I towered over most of the Pakistanis. Feeling gawky, I looked at the ground to avoid stares when we left the hotel, meeting the eyes of children with missing limbs, twisted bodies and outstretched hands begging for coins. Everywhere, men were cleaning up the debris and repairing damaged buildings while overflowing canals slowly drained water from flooded streets to the Bay of Bengal.

The still intact InterContinental Hotel, our temporary home where my father was already settled, swarmed with reporters like locusts in a feeding frenzy, covering the disaster that killed over 300,000 people. My mother recognized some journalists who had covered the India-Pakistan War of 1965 when we lived in West Pakistan. Though it had been five years, a couple of them nodded back in recognition. Many of the news reports were critical of the feeble government disaster response initiated by Lahore-based President Yahya Khan, saying that most of the aid was provided by groups from other countries and that Yahya was largely absent, busy with a trip to China. Dad said he heard his Bengali coworkers grumbling about how West Pakistan siphoned off profits from East Pakistan resources and left them stranded in the aftermath of the catastrophe. He sensed that the physically divided country had deeper divisions than he had been aware of when we lived in Lahore. West Pakistan identified more with the Middle East, whereas the people of East Pakistan thought of themselves as Bengali, like their Indian neighbors, and had strong cultural ties with Southeast Asia. A major issue was language. The attempt to make Urdu the national language did not go over well with the Bengali-speaking East Pakistanis.

Returning to a part of the world he was familiar with from his tours in Afghanistan and Pakistan, Dad was eager to work with colleagues he knew from previous posts at IECo. Plus, he had been promoted to Chief

Engineer for the Karnafuli Irrigation and Muhuri River Projects and had a boss who gave him a lot of responsibility from the start. Mom was thrilled to be living overseas, no matter what the location. I couldn't believe my luck—the move allowed me an easy out, leaving behind the overwhelming adult problems of my junior high school friends in San Francisco. We were all filled with the excitement of possibility.

When we told California friends we were moving to Dacca, no one knew where it was. Not understanding the unusual geopolitical borders, when they learned we were returning to Pakistan, they assumed we were going back to Lahore. Yes, we were going to the same country. No, they weren't close together, being separated by one thousand miles of India between East and West Pakistan. No, we didn't think it was dangerous—our previous military evacuation had been for a minor border skirmish. When we lived in Lahore, we were on the west side of India in the Punjab region, with Afghanistan as a neighbor. Now, we were on the east side of India in the Bengal region, next to Burma (now known as Myanmar), another country carved from India. The newness of Pakistan, only twenty-three-years old, combined with the youthful energy of ladder-climbing young diplomats, engineers, agricultural advisors, and other expats working on well-funded projects, resulted in a pervasively upbeat attitude that quickly drew Mom and Dad into the international community.

HOTEL & CITY

Dacca was even better than I dreamed. Not the city, but the hotel living. The city was a damp, gritty cacophony of rickshaw, bus, car, and motorcycle horns mixed with the blaring call to prayer five times a day over loudspeakers. Open sewers, rotting vegetation, and damp soil from the floods created a stench that took some getting used to. However, we moved into the sleek, stylish InterContinental Hotel, which I embraced with glee. The InterCon, as we called it, became our home in the up-and-coming Shahbag District, sandwiched between Old and New Dacca, and the site of several important universities, gardens, and public spaces. A friend of Dad's, a fishery expert on assignment, said, "The InterCon is like a luxury liner floating in a cesspool of smelly sewage."

When I walked into the high-ceilinged lobby with tile floors, I immediately spotted the gift shop with tempting books in a display carousel. While Dad retrieved the key from the front desk, I peeked at the blue waters of the pool, glittering in the sunlight, beckoning me to take a dip. I vowed to get in as soon as possible. Dad called and we made our way to our room. He opened the door, and I saw only one bed and wondered where my cot was. When Dad was with us, I always had a cot in their room. Dad opened another door and ushered me through it. Startled to see an identical room with a bed, desk, and bathroom, I couldn't comprehend what I was seeing.

"This is your room," he said, leaving me speechless. My own hotel room? All thoughts of the pool vanished temporarily. What a fabulous thirteenth birthday present—my own room, just like an adult. "We'll keep the door open, so you won't be scared. We'll be right here." Scared? I wasn't scared. I loved it. I loved everything about the InterCon. I loved having my own bathroom, the bookstore where I spent my allowance, ordering Mulligatawny soup or tikka skewers from the menu, and the pool where I swam every day with schoolmates. I loved hotels, books, and swimming, and life couldn't get much better. I felt like a puzzle piece that fit exactly in this space.

One day, I stood in front of the wire kiosk in the gift shop, reading all the paperback book titles through yellowed cellophane. "We're going to increase your allowance so you can buy a book at the gift shop every week. We don't have a refrigerator full of books this time," Mom said.

"Can I get one right now?" I spun the kiosk around even faster, the titles swirling by in a cloud of letters. "I don't know any of these authors. They seem like grown-up books."

"They are, but you've read adult books before and I think you'd like Agatha Christie. Her private investigator is like that Harriet the Spy you like so much. We can share and I'll read them, too." She was right. I scrutinized Hercule Poirot's techniques, despite not having a clue how to pronounce either of his names. Living in a hotel was the perfect fishbowl to eavesdrop on tête-à-têtes and analyze sartorial details like a detective. After we read every Agatha Christie book in stock, the kiosk looked empty except for some more serious books by Leon Uris. I dove into those, transfixed by the intensity of his writing and the struggles of his characters as they endured the horrors of the Holocaust. The vivid images of mass migrations of people grappling to find religious freedom staggered my malleable mind, and I understood more about how Partition, that terrible act which divided Muslims from Hindus when Pakistan was formed, could have come about. The lighthearted techniques of the child spy and dapper investigator contrasted with this somber side of life.

Dad was in and out of town visiting Chittagong, one of the major job sites, and other areas where they were conducting irrigation feasibility studies during this time of overabundance of water. Unlike arid Northern Peru, where water was lacking, here the focus was on flood control and pump drainage during monsoonal deluges with a goal of increasing rice production from one crop a year to two or three crops a year. His new boss, Mr. Hsu, couldn't have been more different from his manager in Peru, with a hands-off style that suited Dad, and Dad worked well with Mr. Bradshaw, one of the project managers he became friends with. Mom met some women through a social club, especially enjoying the company of Indian and Bengali women who shared recipes and tips on where to find the best fabrics and tailors as they shared news and rumors that they heard from their household staff, husbands, and *Time* and *Newsweek*.

SCHOOL

Riding through the crowded streets in the taxi taking me to school, the driver blasting the horn while swerving violently to avoid cows, became a normal daily occurrence. I sat in the backseat with my hand on my bookbag next to Mom, ready to leap out when we pulled into the crowded driveway where cars and rickshaws disgorged children of all ages at my school in the Dhanmondi residential area. The novelty of going to school in a taxi and the school being in two houses made my ninth school memorable. The elementary school was housed in a building separate from the junior high and high school I attended. My eighth-grade class had twenty students, but the senior class only had four, perhaps because many parents sent the older kids to boarding schools in Europe or the U.S.

The first day, we met with an administrator in a room on the first floor—was that the parlor or the dining room? I couldn't tell. After I was registered, I climbed the stairs to my first class in what had been a bedroom. I did a condensed version of the name game, clarifying that I went by my middle name. I chatted eagerly with the other kids sitting around me, earning the usual rebukes on my report cards that I was a social butterfly. Conversations with classmates usually followed a script.

"Where have you lived before?"

"What kind of school did you go to?"

"How long is your dad's posting?"

"Where are you going next?"

I found that many of the kids had arrived in Dacca within the past year and were open and welcoming. Some of the older kids were going on relief missions to help hard-hit areas of the cyclone, adult actions that seemed very mature to me, but in a different way than my classmates in San Francisco who were pregnant and doing drugs. At birthday parties here, we listened to the Beatles or classmates who formed a band and drank orange Fanta. Almost all of us were veterans of other foreign schools, some having attended boarding schools, others going to international or American schools like this one, a few experiencing correspondence schools like Calvert. Hardly anyone mentioned US locations, instead rattling through all their overseas posts like a junior United Nations' delegation: Egypt, Thailand, Philippines, Algeria, and India, among others.

REPORTERS

Months later, long after Cyclone Bhola exhaled its last gasp, the journalists remained.

"Why are you here? There can't be that much cyclone news anymore," Mom said to a journalist at the InterCon.

"No, not the cyclone directly. When we were covering the cyclone, we heard how unhappy the Bengalis were with Yahya, but it was low-level grumbling. Just as we were packing up, he called for the elections to proceed as if the cyclone never happened, even though the place is still in shambles. Then the anti-Pakistan rhetoric really ramped up. It looked like a Nationalist movement was strengthening. Now the question is, what is going to happen to the country? Is it going to remain one country or split in two? So, we stayed."

Mom was shaken when she relayed the news to Dad. "What do you think will happen?"

"No one knows, but Yahya will keep a tight rein on the people, so after the election, it will settle down. The official word is there's nothing to worry about."

It was an enormous shock when the charismatic Sheikh Mujib Rahman of the Awami League, based in East Pakistan, won the election instead of Yahya Khan, and there were endless discussions in the papers and around the dinner table about how the ruling party in West Pakistan was going to react. Things got complicated when the ruling military junta didn't invite Sheikh Mujib, whose platform was based on more representation for East Pakistan, to form a government, as was customary.

The articles published in international newspapers from the journalists we knew and gossip among the expats was that the military-controlled government of West Pakistan was ready to quash the East Pakistani Bengali nationalist movement, no matter what it took. More disturbing were the reports that the US supplied Sabre jets, Chaffee tanks, and jeeps with mounted machine guns, but US President Nixon kept downplaying the situation in East Pakistan, saying Yahya could resolve the issues relatively peacefully and keep the country intact. It was under this cloud that we moved into our new house in the upscale Gulshan neighborhood.

HOUSE

Weeks earlier, I had told Mom, "I love living at the InterCon. This is the best assignment we've ever had. Having all the journalists and diplomats around makes it exciting and I get to see all my new friends at the pool."

"Don't get too used to it. We'll be moving soon," she said curtly.

"What? I'd rather stay here. I thought construction of our new house would take longer."

"Too bad. We need to get into a house and get back to normal life. You're living in a fantasy world here." I knew it was too good to last.

Mom and Dad talked incessantly about how to furnish the house, dragging me along to furniture builders, fabric stalls, and streets lined with housewares, but I kept hoping for more construction delays. My parents complained about the unchanging and well-sampled InterCon menu selections, the lack of space in their hotel room, and the limited clothing selections in their closet, closely monitoring the arrival of our shipment from the States. I, on the other hand, had settled into the hotel like a bird in her perfect feathered nest. I had everything I needed in my hotel room.

A white concrete wall with an iron gate enclosed our new house. An emerging garden wrapped around the house on the sides and back, with servants' quarters set apart from the main house. Fragrant frangipani perfumed the air, and fruit-laden mango, papaya, and banana trees added a sweet ambrosia. Small, bright green barbets flitted from blossom to blossom while larger black spotted koels pecked at rotting mangos littering the ground Next door, a wealthy Urdu-speaking Bihari man and his wife moved into a whitewashed house covered in a riot of pink bougainvillea blossoms. We had a large screened-in porch that caught the cool evening breezes. Unlike other Americans who shipped their heavy, dark wooden furniture and wool rugs from home, mom furnished our house with local woven rattan, teak furniture, and cotton rugs that arrived on heavy carts with huge creaking wooden wheels. She scoured the markets for decorative items, hanging a large carved fish from the ceiling, and embellishing the rooms with woven baskets and pounded metal bowls while we waited for our *almirah* closets to be built.

In Lahore, Mom hadn't known the ropes, so she'd followed recommendations from others about the servants to hire. This time, on her third overseas tour, she knew what she wanted—minimal staff and a cook who prepared local foods, not British or American food. And she would hire them, not Dad. A stream of prospective helpers soon arrived to be interviewed.

Handing her their cherished paper chits with valuable handwritten references from previous jobs, the oldest yellowed sheets tattered and worn with threadbare creases, the newer ones crisp and stiff, they would say with their clipped British accent, "Good morning, memsahib. You can see that I have worked for the very best English ladies. I can cook all the special British dishes, roast lamb, mint sauce, cakes, pies, and pastries."

"Tell me what you and your family like to eat," Mom would ask.

"Oh, no, those wouldn't be good enough for you, but I can make an excellent pot roast, or maybe you like spaghetti?"

"No, I'd like to eat Bengali food. Please tell me what you could cook using food from your market." Some stuttered and couldn't seem to remember any of their favorite foods. Finally, Abdul and Rina, a young newlywed couple, came for an interview. They had only a couple of chits. Abdul wished to be a cook and Rina would clean the house.

"Abdul, what Bengali food can you cook for us? What do you like to cook?"

"Certainly, memsahib, do you like fish? We have very good fish in Bengal," he said, rolling his "r"s and referring to the original region, not the current name of the country.

"Yes, I love fish."

"Perhaps a tasty fish curry or crispy grilled fish?" He cupped his hands to show a platter-sized fish. "You will like it."

"That sounds delicious. Will you make chapatti? My husband likes his bread."

"Yes, of course, Rina and I will make you chapatti every day. We will go to the market early each morning when the freshest vegetables are available, and we will make fresh chutney."

Mom hired Abdul and Rina on the spot. They moved their modest bundle of belongings into the small apartment in the back. Mom also hired a *chowkidar* (night watchman), *mali* (gardener), and driver. This was a much smaller staff than most other expat families had and among the Westerners, we were probably at the bottom rung, below the diplomats and oil executives, based on the grand imposing houses I saw. As in Lahore and Piura, Mom didn't want a large staff underfoot that needed to be managed; she wanted the bare minimum to ease the burden of daily shopping in multiple open-air markets, cleaning the house, doing laundry with a wringer washer, hanging clothes to dry, maintaining the garden, and guarding the property. The cost was a fraction of what it would be in the States, and we were respectful of their services and customs, recognizing how fortunate we were to have hired help. On their days off, Mom cooked, made bread, baked pies, and did her canning. Sometimes Dad made fried chicken on Sunday nights, just like he did when we lived in California. I wasn't off the hook with chores. Mom expected me to keep my room neat, set the table, and clear the dishes.

Abdul prepared spicy, fragrant local foods such as dal soup, served as a first course every day at lunch. He made crispy whole grilled fish, as promised, along with fish baked in banana leaf and fish curry with aromatic spices. His pungent yellow chicken curry had a runny sauce, so it was almost soupy, melding with the rice and saturating it with flavor in contrast with the thick curry sauce of the Punjab. He and Rina fired up the small hibachi grill outside the kitchen door to make chapattis, always smiling and chattering together. In the afternoons, when all their chores were done, they would sit on the soft grass under the banana tree while Rina, graceful in her colorful sari, massaged Abdul's feet with perfumed oil. After a few months, Rina's swelling belly gave way to a baby girl. They were so in love and ecstatic to start their family.

Abdul's food was mouthwatering, but Dad still had a taste for treats from home, including such favorites as Spam and pork and beans, tastes he had acquired from his time on PT boats in the South Pacific in World War II. Diplomat's wives sometimes invited us to the commissary, which we didn't usually have access to, or we'd find special imported foods at a small store down the street. We never knew what we'd find there and if they didn't have something we wanted, such as a tin of herring or jars of English mustard, we could ask for it. Mom marveled over their efficiency and wondered where they could order specialty items so fast.

"Abdul, we're out of butter. Could you go to the store and get some? See if they have a few tins of New Zealand butter."

Upon his return, he said. "Memsahib, they are out of butter, but I will go tomorrow, and they will have it, I promise." The next morning, he returned with a single tin of butter.

"Dorothy, you know where that came from, don't you?" said Dad.

"They must have a warehouse somewhere."

"The warehouse is any house where a Westerner lives. They have a network of suppliers, and someone's godown is short one stick of butter today."

Mom chuckled. She had no idea that servants were running a side business out of their employer's pantries. We could get anything—soy sauce, Jell-O, canned ham, chocolate, or just about anything else.

Mom had a small recipe book that went around the world with us. It had her canning recipes, and I'd help her on pickle days. We'd slice and ice the deep green cucumbers, then slice the yellow onions into rings until big tears dripped from our eyes. Then we'd heat the giant vats of water.

My special time with dad was in the late afternoon on the weekend when we'd watch Big Sky during the one hour of English-language programming on our black-and-white TV and eat a special snack of sliced Spam, pickles, and pork 'n beans with a chapatti.

UNREST

Two of my friends, Bobby and Mark, were sons of one of Dad's colleagues.

who lived in the same neighborhood. Most of my new school friends lived too far away to hang out spontaneously. The boys and I spent a lot of time together, being driven to school by one or the other of our family's drivers, doing homework at my house, or playing in our enclosed garden. They were several years younger, so they went to elementary school, a couple of doors down from my junior high. They were rough and tumble, always wrestling each other, or chasing each other. When we were being driven to school, they egged the driver to go faster and faster, which he did, getting us in trouble when another parent saw us as we sped down the main road to school. I tried to keep up with their antics, but despite me being older, they were stronger and always in sync since they played together all the time. They tolerated me, but they were a tight duo and didn't need me for any of their games.

They looked like they could have been my brothers, as we had a similar shade of light brown hair, though theirs was shorn close to their head, while mine was tied back in a ponytail. We dashed on sturdy legs to a nearby park where we were allowed to go by ourselves. We'd run through the opening in the low wall surrounding the park toward a cluster of broad leafy trees, first Bobby, then Mark, then me, trailing behind. After sitting on the grass for a too-brief moment to cool off, we'd toss a ball or chase small lizards into cracks in the wall.

One time, the boys stayed with us for a week when their parents were away. One day, the school called Mom during school hours and told her the boys were missing, but not to worry, they had people out looking for them. Mom informed them that the boys had just arrived at our house, having walked over five miles. It surprised me to see Mom and the boys when the driver picked me up. I was still at school; why weren't they? "What are you doing with my mom? Did you get sick and go home early?"

"No, we walked home."

"That's impossible," I said.

"No, we had it all worked out. We tried to find you, but we didn't know which classroom you were in. A bunch of soldiers went by, and we heard a big bang, so we thought we should tell your mother. We always know how to get home in case we have to walk, and we had a map." Mom shrugged.

"They made it here safely and they had water and snacks with them." I had to admit that they had a well-thought-out plan, and that Harriet the Spy would be proud. But I could never piece all the roads together in my mind when the car whizzed through the streets. I thought they were awfully brave. I asked Mom later if she was mad at the boys, but she said since she hadn't known they were missing, she never had a chance to be worried and since they were safe, she couldn't be mad at them. She turned to the boys. "I guess if your mother walked halfway across a country, it's not so hard to imaging walking across a city," referring to a story about their mother who had escaped persecution in a Middle Eastern country (I was never sure which one), by disguising herself as a man and walking to a neighboring country. She looked sternly at me. "Don't try anything like walking home from school by yourself or you'll be in big trouble."

The next week, at the park, we languidly tossed the ball in the heat of the afternoon, running to look over the wall when we heard the rumble of a heavy truck in the distance. We stood side-by-side at the edge of the lawn and silently watched several military convoys go by. The green jeeps were filled with West Pakistani soldiers in green uniforms and stern faces. I thought of similar scenes I had seen in Lahore five years earlier. I looked at the boys. "What do you think?"

"Looks scary. Why are they pointing those guns at us?" said Bobby.

"We'll be OK," said older brother Mark. "We can take care of ourselves."

"How?" I asked.

"I'll figure something out. We can always walk to a safe place," said Mark. I wasn't so sure, but I knew Mark felt responsible for his little brother.

"We'd better get back," I said, suddenly conscious of my responsibility as the oldest child in the group. They might be faster and stronger, but they didn't always show good judgment, and it was time to go home.

We told Mom what we had seen, excitedly chattering over each other, each adding more details we remembered. She listened intently but just said, "It was probably nothing. Maybe the soldiers were just doing training exercises. Let's go make some popcorn." But I noticed that when Dad came home, she took him into the bedroom and closed the door. All I could hear were low murmurs.

One day I was reading in a balloon chair on the porch, the broad, rattan back swooping into a wide curve behind my head, screening me from view from the outside. Abdul hung a flag on the wall by the guava tree, heavy with ripe fruit, just as the neighbor walked by. He shouted at Abdul, who quickly returned the verbal jabs with escalating fist clenching and jabs at the air. I couldn't understand their rapid-fire Bengali exchange, but they were clearly angry. After they had each stormed away in opposite directions, Abdul shouted, "*Joy Bangla*," which translates to "Hail, Bengal." I looked at the green flag with a red disc. In the middle was the yellow outline of East Pakistan. It was the flag of the liberation movement.

It became increasingly common to see soldiers carrying large firearms standing in groups at street corners and driving around in pickup trucks, the men in the back pointing machine guns at passersby. As the unrest in East Pakistan escalated, I felt uneasy and my stomach churned. Dad kept saying it might blow over. He heard from some friends that President Nixon supported Yahya Khan, and that West Pakistan would get it all sorted out, but Dad sounded skeptical. I worried that if it got as bad as it did when we lived in Lahore, we could be evacuated again. I didn't want to leave this place—I liked it here where I was making friends who were just like me. No one thought my name was odd and all the kids knew where other countries were or had lived in the same places I had. Surely the president of the United States knew more than Dad. Maybe the turbulence would die down soon.

9

The Birth of a Country

BANGLADESH

Thunder boomed in the distance.

"Inga, wake up," my father said one night, shaking me gently. "Hurry. I think the war has started. Get dressed."

That thunder was cannon fire. I sat up quickly and reached for my clothes, straining to hear Dad's quiet words to Mom behind their closed door. What was I dressing for? Were we going to the airport? A friend's house? Running away on foot? Where were my shoes? I couldn't think straight. Matching the rapid pops of gunfire in the distance, my heart banged in my chest.

Mom came into my room just as I found my shoes.

"It was a mistake. Your dad looked at the calendar and it's March 23— Pakistan Day, and that was a twenty-one-gun salute for Independence Day. Go back to bed."

Relieved, I flung myself down next to Chuz and tried to go to sleep in my daytime clothes, but every nerve vibrated with fear. My heart continued thumping, and my thoughts were scrambled like mushy eggs. The signs of increasing military readiness had been obvious for weeks, but we had never talked about a plan. Uniformed men holding rifles or clubs stood on street corners as convoys of tanks moved around the city. I didn't even recognize the grassy area in the park where the boys and I used to play. Now it was dotted with canvas tents and army trucks in a makeshift military camp.

Two nights later, on March 25, 1971, my mother jolted me awake with "Take your pillow and get into the dressing room, now." I hadn't relaxed since the false alarm, so I woke instantly.

"This time it's real. This means the war is starting," said Dad.

I followed the new plan, however flimsy it felt in the moment. No need to dress for unknown journeys, just a short dash into the dressing room, deemed the safest place in the house. I wished I could escape the fear, but the thick walls couldn't block the random pops filling the air, so different from the evenly spaced twenty-one-gun salute of a couple of days before. Surely someone would do something to stop this by morning. But who? The police? The army? The US Government? I realized how little I knew about how the world worked, despite having lived in different countries.

In the tiny dim dressing room next to my parents' bedroom, I lay on a thin mattress. I tried to control my hyperactive breathing, attempting to find a cadence to the rat-a-tat sounds of gunfire. Mom and Dad could fit next to me in the narrow space, but Dad rarely slept, instead he restlessly paced through the house. My mother tucked a blanket around me and dozed, while my father ducked below the windows when shots rang out. I pretended to sleep and even drifted off now and then, hoping that when I woke, it would be over. Every time I heard the buzz of a fighter jet overhead or the heavy rumble of an armored tank, my eyes flew open, and my nerves vibrated like strings on a bass cello. What was that shaking? Did a bomb land close to home? No, it was just my body trembling.

An endless, restless night left us stumbling around the house like zombies the next day. Was it just my imagination or was the call to prayer a little tentative that morning? Work and school were cancelled. Dad took Abdul's flag down because any liberation flags would identify us as friendly to the liberation movement, thus traitors to West Pakistan. Soldiers in green military jeeps rode through the streets with rifles and bullhorns, announcing a strict curfew, one where anyone caught outside past curfew could be shot on sight. When curfew lifted for four hours, between 2:00 and 6:00 PM, we raced to the bazaar to pick up as much rice and canned food as we could find. Mom filled the bathtubs in case they shut the water off. In the afternoon, I sat on my bed half-heartedly doing homework. Would there be a school to turn it into? A big bang sent me sprawling across the bed, papers flying as I slithered to the floor like a snake. I looked through the door to my parents' room and met Mom's eyes as she crouched by their bed.

"What was that? Are they inside the compound? It sounded close," I whispered, envisioning soldiers inside the walls of our property.

"Stay down." Mom waved her hand toward the floor.

We heard metal clattering and Rina appeared, mop and bucket in hand, startled to see us on the floor. She had just dropped the metal pail on the tile floor, but it had sounded like gunshots to us. Sheepishly, we rose as Mom said, "I guess we're a little gun shy." She gave me a hug and said, "This is hard, but we're safe." I ached for everything to return to normal.

A tiny black-and-white TV beamed one English-language show into our house each night. Dad and I loved the American shows, which rotated through *Big Valley, The Wild Wild West, Gunsmoke,* and *The Three Stooges,* giving us an hour's respite from the war. Mom cared more about the news, anxious to learn something about the fighting.

Each night a young man with Bengali-accented English read the news in a thirty-minute broadcast. Eager and bright, he'd read the ten-minute report three times, once each in Bengali, English, and Urdu. As the days passed and the war heated up, he looked worse and worse. At first, he just seemed tired and expressionless, then the spark went out of his eyes as the propaganda escalated about how order was being restored. The words became monotonous and useless. It bothered me, but I couldn't stop watching. His face appeared puffy to me and then, one day, he had bruises. I couldn't stop watching, despite being filled with dread. He had been a lifeline to the outside world and his familiar presence comforted me—the longer it went on, the closer I felt to him. A couple of days later, he appeared with visible cuts. He had two black eyes, and his face was so swollen he could barely talk. The next day, another newscaster sat in his seat reading the news and we never saw the young man again. I felt sick. Leon Uris had filled my head with stories about the Holocaust so I could easily fill in the blanks. Mom tried to come up with plausible explanations for what had happened—maybe he had had a few days off, or he had been fired, or transferred. I knew better. Leon Uris had told me. His accounts of World War II made the machinations of war all too clear in his books.

As the war dragged on day after day, we adjusted to the chilling activity swirling around us. Days were usually quiet as tanks were re-positioned on the riverbanks, readying for the nighttime assault on villages on the opposite side of the water. Mom and I stayed inside, but Dad sometimes visited his coworkers at their homes for short periods to pool the rumors they were hearing. I did schoolwork and read, while Mom helped Abdul and Rina in the kitchen.

Throughout the city we could hear bursts of gunfire at night as liberation fighters clashed with the West Pakistan army, who lobbed phosphorus grenades into villages.

One night in the second week, we crept silently up the darkened stairwell to the roof of our house. It was past curfew, and the fighter jets had been flying overhead for hours. I stood outside, feeling the rough concrete with my toes while my eyes adjusted to the dim light. Tiny bats swooped around my head, casting eerie shadows from the moon hanging low in the sky. I leaped back when I felt puffs of warm wind from their wings across my cheeks. I threw my arms over my head, cowering to keep the bats from getting tangled in my long hair.

"Look there," Mom whispered, pointing at a shimmering line of pinpoint lights, not noticing my silent battle with the bats.

"What is it?" I asked, peeking through my crossed arms, momentarily distracted.

"It's people walking to India, probably Hindus," Mom said. I couldn't make sense of this. India was a different country. We were in East Pakistan. You didn't just walk to India. You took a bus, or you flew in an airplane. Or maybe you did walk. I thought of Bobby and Mark's mother walking across a border in her disguise. The hum of bats' wings blended with the drone of fighter jets. Flashes of light lit up the sky from phosphorus grenades launched at thatch-roofed houses like fireworks of terror. The line of refugees never stopped, like a deep river coursing toward an abyss.

"Why Hindus?" I asked.

"We're hearing that it's mostly Hindus that are being targeted by the Muslim-majority West Pakistanis. Along with university students and journalists," said Dad.

"Are we safe?"

"So far, they haven't attacked any Americans." Good to hear, but it sounded flimsy to me. Was it possible that just being Caucasian and having an American passport could save us from danger? Or could that be me, trudging in a long line of refugees, carrying nothing but Chuz?

"What is that awful smell?" asked Mom. The acrid odor hung in the air, like burned charcoal or cigarettes.

"I don't know, but that's enough," said Dad, his voice sounding tight, his arm around my shoulder, firmly guiding me to the doorway. "Time to go downstairs."

The next day, we found out what the bad odor was after Dad visited some friends. He told us mass graves were dug in the football field at the university to bury the professors and students who had been killed in a massacre the night the fighting started. Bodies were being burned in pits that had been dug near our neighborhood. My stomach churned. It seemed unbelievable that this was happening, like a bad dream I couldn't wake from. I quietly digested this news. I didn't want to be in this version of a Leon Uris book anymore. I asked no more questions.

FEAR

A few days later, while listening to The Beatles in my bedroom, I heard a commotion in the front of the house. Opening the door, I saw an army man towering over my father. Forcing a 45-caliber handgun to my father's head made the Major seem like an ominous giant. Mom raced toward me with a wild look in her eye. Whispering urgently, she pointed to my room and said, "Your bathroom, go to your bathroom." It was the next safest place after the dressing room, now blocked by armed soldiers. I ran to the bathroom and lay on the floor. Where, though? Under the window so nobody would see me from outside? Or on the opposite side to be further from bullets flying through the wall? What if bullets came through the window? Where would they hit? Should I lie flat? Maybe crouching would be better? I tried different positions, considering all the angles. My mind whirred like a spinning wheel. Finally, I stretched out in the middle of the floor face down, my cheek against the cold tile, not daring to look up. I kept as still as I could, as if that would protect me. Then I heard a terrible wail—Rina, the cook's wife. Tears rolled down my cheeks as I imagined all kinds of horrors in the servant's quarters. I sat up, pressed my body against the wall and slid up to the window, peeking outside, not expecting to see anything. Rina's wail sounded like it was coming from the servant's quarters. Under the banana tree where Rina used to rub Abdul's feet, near where Abdul got in the argument with the neighbor, just yards from where I used to read my book on the screened porch, stood a soldier holding a rifle, a sidearm strapped to his leg. Everything about my world, my sense of safety, the protection of the wall, shattered like a crystal vase hitting the cold tile. My mom came in to comfort me and we clung to each other, sitting on the floor. "There's a soldier at each corner. They are looking for Abdul."

"Is he here? Did they find him?" I asked.

"No, he's not here. I don't know where he is. Rina is there with her baby."

"Is she OK?"

"I don't know. Stay here. I'm going to check on Dad."

My mind closed down like a raisin, just like it did on the ship in Peru with the bad man. I was awake but suspended in a petrified world where men with guns were far away. A sharp crack cut through the air, piercing my safe cocoon—a gunshot, and close by. They had found Abdul; I knew it. Mom must have been mistaken. I trembled against the cold tile.

Rina and her baby appeared at the door, ushered in by Mom after the soldiers sent them into the main house. We huddled together on the cold floor with tears streaming down our faces as she told me the soldiers attacked their bed, shooting the mattress and stabbing the pillows with bayonets, but finding nothing but kapok stuffing. Abdul wasn't dead because he wasn't there.

A soldier came to the bathroom and beckoned us to follow him into the living room. Once again, the major pointed a gun at Dad's head, and said, "If the cook returns, he's your responsibility. We'll be back at six." They departed, spraying bullets at a bunch of children playing in the street. Miraculously, no one was shot.

A confusing story emerged, a classic tale of neighbors on opposing sides. Following the argument between the Bihari neighbor and Abdul, our cook had told a roving band of liberation fighters that the neighbor supported the West Pakistan military. Abdul and the liberation fighters were members of the Awami League that supported an independent East Pakistan. The neighbor, fearing for his life, reported Abdul to the West Pakistan military police as a traitor. The soldiers were under orders to kill Abdul on the spot. Rina said maybe he had gone back to their village, but no one knew whether the village still existed. Standing in the kitchen, she looked small and forlorn.

Six o'clock came and went. Mom packed a small suitcase and hid it behind the refrigerator in case—what? In case we had to grab it and run? In case they bayonetted all our clothes? In case they ransacked the house? After Dad circled the perimeter of the house at least three times, checking the locks on windows and doors as he had done every night of my life, we went to bed in the dressing room. At midnight, loud banging on the door awakened us. Dad opened the door to find the major there, demanding that we turn over our cook. Dad calmly told him he would hold Abdul if he returned but that he wasn't here, and we didn't know when he'd be back. They checked the servant's quarters, but no one was there, not even Rina. Dad had given her some money and told her to do what she needed to be safe. She had dressed in her best sari and slipped away in the night with their baby.

The next day, after a fitful sleep, I waited for Rina to return and wondered if Abdul would come too. When she didn't come back that day or the next, I asked Mom if she ever would.

"No, she's gone. She said she would join the line of refugees and try to get to India." It hit me hard when I realized I'd never see her again, and I drew a shaky breath. Worry consumed me—we had heard reports of mass rapes of Bengali women by the army.

Abdul might be dead, and Rina was gone. I could see her face and imagine her in that long line of refugees, carrying her baby, her beautiful sari in tatters. That's when the war became real to me.

EVACUATION

Although Mom worried about Abdul and Rina, she was more concerned about how we would get out. Most of the other western countries had evacuated their citizens, but we had heard nothing from the US consulate on when our day would come.

"This is what happened in Lahore, too. My American friends who were evacuated from places said it's always the Americans who are the last to leave. A month ago, other countries started evacuating. Why are we always at the end of the line?" Mom asked.

"I know it seems that way, but we can't do anything until we get the official word. Nixon is still saying everything is under control, so until the government makes the call we're stuck. Maybe the company will try to intervene, but they always want to protect their investment. I have to think about my job, too. We must be patient," Dad said. I listened to this exchange in wonder. There were so many moving parts, and we couldn't decide if we should leave on our own without ramifications.

We packed our bags, one suitcase each, and the heavy silver in the Pan Am bag, so we'd be ready at short notice. Finally, around April 1, 1971, Archer Blood, the U.S. consul general, recommended that U.S. citizens be evacuated, but, like before, the recommendation was only for women and children. We were notified of a possible time frame by a representative of IECo, Dad's company. The families of diplomats were evacuated first, and we had to wait our turn since Dad worked for a private company. That meant we were a lower priority. We heard some employees were evacuated to Bangkok, Thailand and others to Tehran, Iran, but we didn't know if we'd be taken to either one or somewhere different. Mom wept at the prospect of leaving Dad, though he tried to console her.

"Carroll, it's not safe. What if the soldiers come back looking for Abdul?"

"I don't think they'll be back. They wouldn't hurt Americans. They wouldn't want to deal with the reaction from the US if Americans were attacked."

"I know, but can we really count on that? All it takes is one trigger-happy zealot."

"Don't worry. I'll be OK. You make sure you get out with Inga."

I had never heard Mom and Dad talk like that, where they made it so obvious that we were some kind of protected class. I hoped Dad was right, but I worried about the Bengalis, who had no one to protect them when their own government turned on them.

A few days later, a truck full of soldiers drove by our house, spraying bullets randomly. Dad ducked on the front step as a bullet flew over his head into the concrete wall of our house. He ran inside. From then on, we avoided going into the yard or lingering by windows, hoping for our evacuation orders.

"See what I mean, Carroll? Just because we're American doesn't mean a stray bullet can't find a target," said Mom.

"That was close, but they weren't aiming at me. You're right though. I'll feel better when you're safely out of the country."

On the afternoon of April 13, we got word that we were to report to the airport that night. It had been nineteen days since the start of the war.

"You need to get out as quickly as possible. I'll go stay with Bradshaw, along with two other engineers, and we'll leave as soon as we can. It'll be safer if we're together," said Dad.

The drive to the American School, where we were instructed to report to, was strained. We were all nervous about the possibility of getting shot. There were so many reports of random violence of the kind we had seen. At dusk, we were bussed to the airport. Dad came with us on the bus but couldn't join us at the airport. After a quick hug and many tears, Mom and I stumbled to the holding area with bags, grief-stricken to leave Dad behind. Similar scenes were repeated among all the families around us. Mom sniffled and said, "We can do this. We've done this before, and we just have to trust that Dad will be OK. We can be strong, right?"

"Sure, Mom, I can try." I could see that I needed to be tough for Mom. We each shouldered a blue Pan Am bag and picked up our small suitcases. On the tarmac, we could see shadowy, sinister shapes of tanks and other military equipment. Soldiers carrying rifles stood at intervals around the building. We dried our eyes, and Mom took my hand as we walked into the pool of light shining into the parking lot where a vast crowd of expats waited to be processed. Most of my friends had diplomat parents and had already been evacuated. Every nerve was on fire with emotional exhaustion, and it was hours before a Pakistan International Airlines plane descended from the black sky with no lights until the last minute. West Pakistani troops dressed in civilian clothes descended from the plane, marched into a hangar, and emerged in military uniforms.

Finally, at 1:30 am, we boarded the plane and settled into our seats—seats just vacated by the West Pakistan army. The door closed, and the plane lifted off in a dramatically steep ascent in pouring monsoonal rain with lightning all around. I felt a swirl of emotions, glad to be headed to safety, sad to leave my father behind, and aware of our privilege to be evacuated when Rina, Abdul, and millions of East Pakistanis, rich and poor, couldn't get out. Our blue US passport meant everything, the difference between life and death, between choice and impotence. We left Dad, our home, my school, and Pakistan in a vapor trail, this time with my sense of security that the government or Dad's company could keep us safe stripped away.

10

Adolescent Angst
in Marin

TRANSIT

At some point between our sharply angled ascent out of Dacca and our arrival in Karachi, as I tried to find sleep in a thousand impossible positions, Mom and Lola decided to team up on the journey to the States. Among the roiling crowd of expats at the airport, Mom had run into Lola, the wife of one of dad's colleagues, and her two children. Emma was a slim, solemn girl of ten, with thin brown hair that hung limply upon her shoulders and a wispy presence that faded into the furniture. Her two-year-old sister, Lottie, was sturdy, with golden curls and a cherubic face when she wasn't throwing a tantrum.

When the plane took off, I was tense, not knowing if we'd be shot down. After an hour or so, I could relax a little but was worried about Dad and the possibility that he could be shot on his way home. Our route took us all the way around the southern tip of India, and we refueled in Columbo, Ceylon (now Sri Lanka) because airspace over India was restricted due to the war. What should have been a three-hour flight took over eight hours. After landing, I flinched when I heard gunshots. My reflex was to drop to the floor, but I was strapped into my seat. I was confused. Where were we? Had we turned back to Dacca? We were supposed to be flying away from the fighting. The pilot announced that there was an uprising in Ceylon, and there was a skirmish close to the airport. Looking pale and worried, Mom put her arm around me as if to shield me. The plane was refueled so fast there was no time to restock and the only food we got was a stale sandwich and some rotten fruit from a surly flight attendant. After touching down briefly in Karachi, West Pakistan, we flew to Tehran, Iran, where we had been evacuated to from Lahore so many years ago. I was relieved to be out of the war zone and exhausted from the long flight and days of tense lead-up to the evacuation. We still had a long journey ahead, but for now, we needed sleep.

At adult gatherings, Lola had always been the life of the party, the first to have a drink and the first to twirl onto the dance floor. It only took one night to see the flip side of the vivacious, fun-loving Lola. It started with taunts directed at Emma, who took charge of getting her sister ready for bed while avoiding the line of fire and ended with Mom bundling me and the sisters to another room to sleep as Lola got meaner. When Lola finally fell into a drunken sleep, Mom sorted everyone into the correct beds. I understood more about why Emma was so quiet since she took the brunt of her mother's anger, while Lottie could do no wrong. I didn't know what to do. Mom had said traveling with another family would make things easier, but Lola's behavior upset me.

I thought all moms were like mine—too strict sometimes but always keeping their kids safe. I never knew moms could be mean for no reason. When Lola slurred her words and sounded guttural, it scared me, like there was a wild animal sitting inside her, coiled and ready to pounce.

Seated on the sofa with clenched teeth, seething as Lola lobbed another assault at Emma, I longed to disappear. Like a magic trick, poof, gone. Mom snuck extra tonic into Lola's glass to dilute the drink, but when she caught on, she'd grab the gin bottle by the neck and glug it roughly into her glass with unsteady hands. The shots in the glass kept coming, the shots at Emma wouldn't stop.

Like our previous evacuation route out of Lahore during the India-Pakistan War of 1965, we traveled from Tehran to Lebanon, where we showed Lola and the girls around the vibrant city of Beirut and tried to wash away our worries in the hotel pool. Our route through Rome allowed for some rest while we awaited word from the men left behind, hoping they might join us. Being tourists was a relief, the weight of ancient history providing a transitory stability to my world. The grandeur of the massive Coliseum, its solid columns still standing after nearly two centuries, and the solemn, subterranean world of the catacombs with their bones still intact after almost 500 years, gave me the perspective that life goes on despite invasions, wars, and conquests. The elegant, watery world of Villa D'Este, with its fifty-one gravity-fed frothy fountains spraying rainbows into the sky and intricate waterways still murmuring through manicured gardens after 400 years filled my imagination, briefly replacing the brutal images of battle in my mind with those of beauty and grace. My fractured nerves were soothed by the gentle splash of falling water, the solace of the fern-filled moist grottos, and the surprise of hidden statues under clear, blue skies.

MEMPHIS

Telegrams flying back and forth confirmed that the men were to remain in Dacca, so we bid goodbye to our traveling companions, relieved to be away from the volatile Lola, and headed to Memphis, Texas, our usual safety net with my maternal grandparents.

I loved Grandma and Grandad, but they were strict and formal. That terrible tantrum I threw when I was eight still bothered me. No one ever brought it up again, but I still felt deep shame for losing control over an irrational fear that Mom might not come back when she left Grandma to babysit me. Whenever I thought of it, heat flooded my body, and my cheeks burned in embarrassment. To show them how grown up I was now, I tried to always be polite and controlled. Mom, too, seemed more exacting with me when they were around. When I was well-behaved, Grandad would reward me with a bowl of vanilla ice cream smothered in chocolate sauce.

My Uncle John's new wife, Carol, was like no adult I had ever known. Her loving heart was boundless, bigger than the state of Texas, exuding a cloud of warmth and kindness that drew me into her magnetic force field. She could be fun and playful or serious and attentive, and was always ready with a big hug. Her wide, welcoming eyes were like pools of light, receiving me without judgement. I'd share and share some more, including details about my fumbled first kiss in a closet during a teen hide-and-seek game and an awkward moment playing spin-the-bottle, where I embarrassed myself by refusing to remove any clothing when I understood how their version of the game worked. She spent hours listening to my tales of woe as we sipped ice-cold Dr. Pepper. Under her protective cloak of compassion, I felt no problem was insurmountable. John, full of quips and good cheer, made Mom laugh for the first time in months, and Dan, their determined three-year-old, was fun to play with, though, to be honest, I liked it best when he was napping so I could have my aunt to myself.

Added to this was the rekindling of my friendship with Bonita, who lived across the street from my grandparents and had taken me cotton picking after our previous evacuation. This time, we became classmates when Mom enrolled me in Memphis Junior High for the last few months of eighth grade. Bonita tucked me firmly under her wing and took me everywhere with her, explaining Texas slang, football, shaving legs, makeup application, and pimple remedies that were new to me. She gently pushed my hand away when I tried to hold hers on the playground, saying, "Girls don't do that here," and made me a costume that matched hers for a graduation parade, so I'd fit in. I felt, like Harriet the Spy, I was leading a double life. Harriet was a regular schoolgirl by day and ran her missions at night. With Bonita as my guide, my job was to act like a teenager in this bubble of a well-ordered midwestern life, while the real world raged beyond our borders.

I had no idea if I absorbed everything I was supposed to learn in eighth grade, but I was still a year ahead since Mom had started me in first grade a year early, and I wasn't tested this time. This was the most tumultuous year of my complicated school history, with stints in San Francisco, Dacca, and Memphis, but I graduated on time. I supposed I was ready for high school.

The stress of the war, evacuation, and protracted journey back to the States slowly dissipated, becoming less focused. But things were not normal in the other part of my double life.

My grandfather had saved a stack of newspapers with reports of the war. Glancing at the page on top, "Operation Searchlight" jumped out at me. What was that? I had never heard those words in Dacca. I read with interest that this was the name of the military campaign that started on March 25, 1971, that terrifying night when Mom woke me to hide in the dressing room.

I picked up a newspaper and stared at the photos for a long time. I studied one image, seeing up close what I had viewed from afar. Long lines of refugees shuffling toward India, little boys wearing nothing but a ragged T-shirt, a girl my age in a tattered dress, men with thin arms holding bundles on their heads, every single person barefoot. I shuddered to think about what my life would look like if I changed places with that little girl. How I wished I could put them all in a magic vessel to keep them safe, but they were trapped.

I looked at another story, written by Sydney H. Schanberg of the *New York Times*.

> DACCA, Pakistan, March 27 —*The Pakistani Army is using artillery and heavy machine guns against unarmed East Pakistani civilians to crush the movement for autonomy in this province of 75 million people.*

The attack began late Thurs day night without warning.
West Pakistani soldiers, who predominate in the army, moved
into the streets of Dacca, the provincial capital, to besiege
the strongholds of the independence movement, such as the
university.

So, the rumors were true about the University of Dacca being targeted. I read that dozens of university faculty and students were slaughtered that night in a hail of bullets, that two dozen city blocks had been razed, that two newspaper operations were in ruins, that thatch-roofed villages went down in flames. Mass graves were dug on campus, just as Dad had heard. Estimates of student deaths were in the hundreds. My heart thumped in my chest the same way it did that night when I was huddled on the thin mattress. My hands shook; the newspaper rattling uncontrollably. But still, I read on, unable to stop.

Scores of artillery bursts were seen and heard by foreign
newsmen confined to the Intercontinental Hotel on threat of
death.

I was crushed to see the InterCon mentioned in connection with terror, the terror the newsmen must have experienced, in the hotel that had been such a place of refuge for me—that sparkling blue water of the giant pool, the twirling kiosk in the gift shop that held all my favorite books, the airy lobby always full of fascinating journalists.

Reports also said that West Pakistani soldiers were shelling
and burning houses and factories as Awami League volunteers
poured into towns from their villages and attacked the troops.

Those must have been all the villages we saw burning from our rooftop. If Abdul were still alive, he might have been part of those Awami League volunteers fighting for independence. I put the newspaper down for a moment and looked out the window, remembering Abdul and the flames from the burning villages shooting at the sky across the river.

One *New York Times* article headline, dated March 31, reported that Dacca was quiet. Not in our house—that was around the time the army police were ransacking our house. A flood of emotion ran through me as I relived every moment of that episode all the way from running to my bathroom, to lying on the floor with my cheek to the tile, to looking out the window to see the soldier with the bayonet. The terror of that moment flooded back.

In the papers there were estimates that three million or more were killed in the mass genocide, with ten million fleeing to India in those long lines winding through the land. India accepted them, but the refugee camps quickly overwhelmed the services they could provide. There wasn't enough food, clean water, or shelter, but the refugees kept coming.

Folding the newspaper carefully, I placed it back in the pile for Grandad. I couldn't read any more. Needing some fresh air to clear my head, I walked outside, breathing in the warm air, the sun a glowing orb in an impossibly big sky stretching across the cotton fields on the high plains of Texas. I stood in the backyard, fingering the junipers to release their piney scent. The red brick road drew me to the street that was as empty as the sky and I looked into the gorge, a big gash like so many others in this otherwise flat plain, so spacious that it held the large city park in its bosom. The pure song of the cicadas pierced the air with no audible competition. Such a tranquil moment was impossible to imagine on the other side of the world where Dad was.

We were safe, but Dad wasn't. He was still living in a war zone. I was suspended between worlds, trapped in limbo until he could come home.

One night, I overheard my aunt talking to my mother.

"Were you in danger?"

"A little, but it's hard to know how much. Being American helped, but that only goes so far."

"Did anything happen that scared you?"

"One time, a car was driving after curfew in front of our gate. The military police came by and fired shots. Carroll ran out to see what happened, and they shot the driver dead. That was scary because it was so close, and they didn't bother to ask questions." Blood drained from my face, and I felt faint. I remembered that evening, but Dad had said they just shot in the air, like they always did. But maybe they hadn't. Maybe they were always shooting people, not clouds. What else hadn't they told me? What happened to Abdul and Rina? Was Dad going to be able to get out? Was he really with Bradshaw, or was he alone? Was it any better if he was with Bradshaw? When would this end? I gulped some air and sank down to the floor in the hallway where they couldn't see me and buried my head in my hands. There were no answers to any of these questions. I just wanted Dad to come home, for all of them to come home. Tears flowed down my cheeks. I didn't tell Mom what I heard. I knew I had to be strong. For Mom.

* * *

Mom tried to keep things lighthearted, planning little excursions to the park for a picnic, and laughing with her brother and old friends. But when she showed me her ring finger, I knew there was more going on under the surface for her, too. All around her wedding ring, her skin was red, raw, and peeling, just like before. She must have been as tormented as I, not knowing if Dad was in danger, anxiously waiting for telegrams from Dacca, any scrap of information that would set her mind at ease. All her worry was concentrated in her ring finger.

Finally, the telegram arrived with the welcome news that Dad was on his way. I was thrilled and immensely relieved when I knew he'd be with us again, but faced the wrenching realization that I would have to leave my aunt and friends behind in the next move. This time, I knew we probably wouldn't return to Dacca. A sense of panic rose in my chest. I couldn't breathe for a moment, but I knew what was required. Deep breaths. I had to be stoic.

Weeks later, when Dad finally returned, it was a glorious homecoming for me and Mom and the rest of the family. I was so relieved to have him back—the tightness in my chest and all my worry seeped out of my bones like molten lava. His face was drawn, and his eyes didn't seem focused, but maybe that was jet lag. After a few days, he started to engage more and busied himself organizing our move to San Francisco as quickly as possible. It was hard to believe that we went through a whole cycle of the flurry of packing, the excitement of being overseas again, another evacuation, and the agony of repatriation, in less than a year.

MARIN

Shortly after we returned to San Francisco, Dad had some big news.

"We're going to stay in one place for four years. I've decided that I won't accept any overseas transfers, so unless something drastic happens, we'll be here all through your high school."

"Why?" Startled, I could only get that one word out.

"You need some consistency to study and do well. Going to school on two continents and two states in one grade isn't conducive to preparing for college. I talked to my boss at International Engineering Company, and he agreed that I could work at the home office for now."

"But I made it through and graduated from eighth grade on time," I said.

"That's because you're smart, but school is going to get harder, and you'll learn more if we're not moving every few months. Tomorrow, we're going to look for a place to live. We can't live at the Seal Rock Inn forever."

I didn't know what to do with this information. I didn't always like being in the States, but we couldn't go back to any of the other places I remembered unless Dad had a contract to work there. It wouldn't be the same since none of my friends would be there—their fathers also moved around every few years. At least if we had to be in the U.S., San Francisco was familiar.

"I like it here." Of course, I did. I loved living in hotels, and this one was a block away from a house we used to live in, across the street from Sutro Heights Park. Mom's two best friends, who lived nearby, both had kids my age that I got along with.

I had made uninspired, primitive pottery at an art camp at the DeYoung Museum in Golden Gate Park and had a glancing brush with a couple of the kids before we went to Peru. The moms bonded instantly when they picked us up at the end of the first day and had stayed friends ever since. They were experienced world travelers and teased my parents at cocktail parties about the places we had lived when we caught up with them again.

"Dorothy, have you ever noticed that whenever there's a political hotspot or war zone, you happen to be there? Are you sure Carroll is really an engineer?" said Mrs. Merman, one of the moms from the DeYoung Museum.

"Oh, that's funny. Yes, I can assure you that he really is an irrigation engineer, not an undercover agent. Just ask him anything about ditches, canals, and water pumps and he'll be happy to bore you to tears. Right, Carroll?" Dad was mixing a drink and popped an olive in his martini before walking over to them.

"Real jobs can still be a cover, you know. The CIA is clever that way."

"Hold on here. I know it's titillating to spin conspiracy theories, but let's just put a stop to this right now. I'm just a simple farm boy who fell into work with an international company," said Dad in a tone that did not invite banter. An awkward silence followed. "How about those forty-niners? Great football game, right?" said Dad, finishing that conversation. I thought it was funny, but there's no way he was anything but an engineer with IECo.

I was hoping I could go to the same school as my old friends from art camp, thinking I could start school with a built-in friend or two. And maybe I'd find some classmates from Presidio Junior High. Finally, I could go to school where I knew someone, in a neighborhood that was familiar. The high schools nearby drew students from two elementary schools and one middle school I had attended, and when I thought of going to the same school for four years, I pictured being part of a large group of friends. "Will I go to Washington or Lincoln High?"

"Neither. We're going across the Golden Gate Bridge to Marin County to look at houses. The schools are better, and we can get a bigger house. It's still close enough to the city that I can commute to work."

"Whaaat?" I almost fell off my chair. My dreams were dashed—we weren't going to live in San Francisco, where I was already an expert at riding the city bus and could start high school with kids I already knew. I didn't know anything about Marin County. Resigned, I sighed deeply and audibly, exerting maximum teen angst.

The next day we drove across the Golden Gate Bridge in a swirl of dense fog, the brick red spans disappearing into the mist a few feet above the car. After passing through the Waldo Tunnel, Richardson Bay glittered in brilliant sunshine.

Mom pointed at the bay. "Oh, look how beautiful it is. Someday, I'm going to live here, in Sausalito." I couldn't reconcile this from the woman who only wanted to be somewhere else.

"But Mom, you love it overseas and you never want to be back here," I said.

"I know, but when I'm old, I probably won't be able to live over there and if I have to be in the States, this is where I want to be."

"Are we going to live in Sausalito now?"

"No. We can't afford it. But someday . . . " We drove through the charming, seaside town with dense homes dotting the steep slopes above the docks and houseboats lining the bay shore. Mount Tamalpais towered over rolling hills that hugged one suburban neighborhood after another, getting more rural as we went. We passed Sir Francis Drake High School with long, low-slung buildings, airy outdoor hallways, tennis courts and large ball fields—so different from the big imposing brick schools in San Francisco. The best part was the Olympic-sized pool. Maybe the suburbs were okay. We found a house a few blocks away from the school, and I settled into the novel idea of attending one school for four years.

Dad got used to commuting by bus to the IECo office on New Montgomery Street in downtown San Francisco, where he prepared proposals for engineering projects around the world that others would execute. This included a feasibility study for a project in Mexico, and another for the Chakhansur Flood Control and Irrigation Project in Afghanistan, near the Helmand Valley. He was happy to work on this one because that's where he was based during his first overseas engineering post, and he had lots of connections.

Mom decided it was time to put her long-dormant teaching credential to work and signed up to be a substitute teacher for high schools in Marin County. I was amazed to think of Mom having a job and maybe even subbing in one of my classes. Later, she signed up to teach creative cooking classes at the adult education center, creating and testing recipes from around the world each week. I used my new skills from Typing 101 to record her recipes. Dad and I loved this phase where we got Mexican food every day for a week, then Asian food, then Middle Eastern food.

SCHOOL

I had never been to a suburban school before and many of the predominantly white kids had been together since elementary school. Their entire world seemed to be organized around school sports, the mall, and hanging out with lifelong friends.

Sophia, who was an intellectual loner, was one of the few who expressed any interest in where I had lived. I reciprocated by embracing her ornithology passion fully, going on long walks at the end of Sleepy Hollow to roam the grassy, open hills, binoculars in hand, following the graceful red tail hawks and tippy-winged vultures hanging motionless in the updrafts. She always got better grades than me and had a fantastic memory, easily absorbing complex concepts in school. Though she was smarter than I, she always seemed to look up to me for reasons I couldn't understand. She thought I was prettier, and I thought she could be anything she wanted to be, but she never felt like she was good enough. We each found something in the other and she became my best friend. Sleepovers alternated between our houses on many weekends. It was always quiet at my house and a madhouse at hers since she had five siblings who made a lot of noise. I could see that her three brothers got all the attention and special favors from her parents while she and her little sister were clearly not the favored ones. I wondered if that's why Sophia felt inadequate, and I tried to give her lots of recognition for her talents, especially later, when she got a full scholarship to Cornell University in New York to study ornithology.

I made some casual friends in my science class, played the flute in the school band, and joined the swim, gymnastics, and basketball teams. Working hard to fit in, I didn't talk to anyone except Sophia about the war and was a reasonable facsimile of a typical American teenager for a minute.

I always did well in English, and I liked writing. For an essay assignment about challenging times, the other kids wrote about things like the time they struck out in baseball or didn't get onto the cheerleading team. I wrote about the war in East Pakistan. I got an A grade, and my teacher asked me to read the story aloud to the class because, as she wrote on the last page, "this paper will fascinate the class." They were not fascinated, and there was dead silence after my reading. We lived in different worlds. I wrote about more mundane topics after that, not wanting to blow my cover as a regular American teenager.

It was 1971, and I wasn't interested in makeup, but curling irons were all the rage. My hair had a slight wave, which Mom tried to encourage by tying up lengths of hair in socks every night. She'd roll four or five sections of hair around knee socks and tie a knot in them at the level of my neck. These were soft enough to sleep on and in the morning, the ends would be curled. With the curling iron, I could control the curls better. One morning, I held the hot iron in place a little too long, singeing the ends of my hair. That smell of burning protein instantly transported me back to that night in Dacca when we were on our roof, watching the long line of refugees and smelling that terrible scent of burning bodies, the same odor I could smell in my room when my hair burned. Tears trickled down my face as I remembered Rina and Abdul and their baby and all the people who died in those burning villages and refugee camps.

Statistics about the war in East Pakistan were reported on the back pages of the newspaper in small clips, and no one—outside of our family—spoke of it. It was an invisible war. The Vietnam War, on the other hand, was highly visible, with extensive reporting and violent demonstrations across the country. The war in East Pakistan was still raging, refugees were still pouring into India, hundreds of thousands of Bangladeshi women had been raped and a large part of the intellectual elite had been murdered.

> *"I saw Hindus hunted from village to village and door to door, shot off-hand after a cursory 'short arm inspection' showed they were un-circumcised. I have heard the screams of men bludgeoned to death in the compound of the Circuit House in Comilla. I have seen truckloads of other human targets and those who had the humanity to try to help them hauled off for disposal under the cover of darkness and curfew."*

Anthony Mascarenhas,
London's *Sunday Times*, June 13, 1971

I was perplexed about why President Nixon seemed to be supporting the West Pakistanis, and it didn't make sense when he sent the USS *Enterprise* from Vietnam to the Bay of Bengal in early December to evacuate US citizens—what citizens could possibly be left? It didn't matter, though.

Suddenly, everyone knew about Bangladesh from an unlikely source. George Harrison, lead guitarist for the Beatles, released a single called "Bangla Desh" and organized a charity concert that drew 40,000 people to two shows in Madison Square Garden on August 1, 1971. The publicity from the concert, resulting triple album, which won a Grammy, and concert film, put the war on the map and gave it a face for many people. After that seismic event, any time I mentioned Bangladesh, there was recognition and empathy. I was bewildered that an artist had the power to lift the war out of obscurity for so many people, but it did make it easier for others to at least recognize the name of the country.

By December, India was involved in the war and wiped out the Pakistani air force within two days. On December 16, the West Pakistan army signed surrender papers, and the East Pakistan name vanished. Bangladesh was officially a nation. I never found out what happened to Rina and Abdul.

> *"From the banks of the great Ganges and the broad Brahmaputra, from the emerald rice fields and mustard-colored hills of the countryside, from the countless squares of countless villages came the cry. "Victory to Bengal! Victory to Bengal!" They danced on the roofs of buses and marched down city streets singing their anthem* Golden Bengal.*"*
>
> Time Magazine
> The World: Bangladesh:
> Out of War, a Nation Is Born,
> December 20, 1971

I wondered where my DASS friends were and what kind of schools they were going to. I so wished I could have talked to them about the war. They would understand how I felt. I didn't have anyone's stateside or permanent address. Who had a permanent address, anyway? We always had to use my grandparents' address in Texas.

In my sophomore year, as the leaves were dropping and temperatures were crisping, I was practicing the piano, despite a lack of any obvious talent. Mom walked in and said she wanted to talk to me. I stopped the metronome and spun around on the polished wooden piano bench.

"Your father and I don't think you're getting the right education to prepare you for college at Drake."

"You must be joking. You mean after all the moving around and attending all kinds of schools and dodging wars, now you're worried about regular school out here in the bland U.S. suburbs?"

"I've been talking to some of the other moms who think Marin Catholic has a more rigorous approach." Her face was arranged as if some decision had already been made, with muscles tense and no smile.

"But we're not Catholic. I'm not even sure we're Presbyterian. When's the last time we went to church?" I couldn't remember. Could she?

"You don't have to be Catholic to attend the school. I've already checked on that."

"You've already talked to them?" The noose was tightening.

"Yes, and they say you're an excellent candidate."

"I thought I was going to go to one school for four years. What about that?" I was outraged at this betrayal and wanted to scream, but I tried to remain calm. Maybe I could talk my way out of this.

"Sorry about that. We thought that would work."

"What if I don't want to go?"

"Just try it for a year. We've already paid the tuition, and you'll start in January."

"In the middle of the year? That's horrible. I'll be the new kid again."

"Don't be silly. You've been the new kid so many times that you're a pro. You'll make friends there and you can still see Sophia." I could see that the decision had been made. I was going to another new school to be another new kid and have to make another set of friends.

"It's not the same. You're ruining my life." Storming into my room, I slammed the door with a ferocious kick. I tried to funnel all the power I could muster into the slam, but it was impotent. I was powerless. Why was I an only child? Sophia had four siblings, and her parents barely noticed her. Why couldn't I have that?

A couple of weeks later, as the Christmas tree went up, a big box arrived. I grabbed the scissors to cut the tape around the flat cardboard box. "Is it a present from Grandma?"

"Let's open it," said Mom.

I recoiled when I saw the contents. It was not a present. It was the ugliest plaid skirt I had ever seen, a pleated light blue and black plaid pattern on white. She lifted it up. "Isn't it pretty? It's your new school uniform."

Bursting into tears, I ran to my room and slammed the door harder than ever, diving into my pillow to stifle the sobs. I felt an impotent rage that had no outlet. I looked at my wall calendar for the following year and flipped the pages for each month. So many pages to go until I could be on my own and make my own decisions. I was so mad. I understood why we moved so much when it was for dad's work, but this didn't have anything to do with work and I didn't agree with their reasons.

By January, when I had to don the ugly uniform and enter the stucco building, I resigned myself to the new school, my twelfth since first grade. It was a small school with classrooms arranged around an open-air courtyard lined with benches and lockers. The library and administrative offices were in front, classrooms in the back, and there a chapel and gymnasium were on the property. To go with the hated skirt, Mom had carefully matched a series of white, blue, and black tops with rounded baby doll collars, but I immediately felt out of place, like the prim schoolgirl I was, while the popular girls looked like models from the waist up, wearing all the latest fashions and colors on top, no matter how they clashed with the plaid skirt.

I tried to make friends, but although the girls would say "hi" or smile as we put our books away for lunch, nobody invited me to sit with them and if I wandered over to talk to someone I knew, they never made room on the narrow benches. It was even worse than Drake. The Catholic school system was much smaller than the public schools, so these kids had been in each other's classrooms their whole life and were like a big extended family who didn't need any new members. They didn't see many students entering the system, and certainly not in January.

Eventually, I had to admit that maybe Mom and Dad were right about one thing. The schoolwork was interesting, and I had to up my studying game. Taking Latin, learning Spanish rather than relying on what I picked up in Peru and penning creative writing essays made me enthusiastic and stimulated to learn more. Math even made sense once I got into the right class following a minor disaster when I landed in an advanced math class that was over my head. I had extra time at lunch, since I wolfed down my sandwich by myself and headed straight to the library, my safe space. Surrounded by books, wonderful books, rows of books with spines that reached out to me with enticing titles, I sank into the comfortable silence, the librarians nodding at me as they became familiar with my routine. I did homework or browsed the stacks or read a book. Pearl S. Buck was a revelation, and I marveled at the similarities in our expat backgrounds—she was a Calvert Correspondence School student, just like me, but she endured many more hardships as the daughter of a poor missionary in China. Her stories of Chinese life in the early 1900s captivated me and felt familiar, like going home.

* * *

"Why don't you invite some of your friends over to the house someday? Wouldn't they like to swim?" Mom was looking at me quizzically at the kitchen table one afternoon.

"I don't have any friends."

"Surely you must. You talk about some girls and what they are wearing."

"That doesn't mean anything."

"Well, think about it." This conversation repeated several times. One day, Mom asked who I ate lunch with.

"No one. I eat my sandwich and go to the library afterwards."

Mom had a worried look but asked no more questions. When Dad came home, she told him about it, and they disappeared into the bedroom to talk.

For my December birthday, when I had been at Marin Catholic for an entire year without making a single friend, I blew out the candles on my chocolate cake that Mom had made. I secretly wished time would jump forward to when I could go to college and be on my own.

Mom cut the cake and handed me a big slice. "We have a surprise for you. In January, you're going back to Drake for the rest of your junior year and next year."

It took me a minute to process her words. "Really? I can't believe it, I don't understand, oh, thank you, I'm so happy. I have to call Sophia right now." With words tumbling from my lips, I bolted from the table without even taking a bite of cake and ran to the princess phone in my bedroom. Sophia and I rejoiced at this unexpected turn of events. I went back out to find Mom and Dad sitting with satisfied grins.

I picked up my fork. "What made you change your mind?"

"You didn't have any friends. That's never happened before. You can enroll in advanced placement classes at Drake, and you're smart enough for college." Relief flooded my body as the news sank in. I felt like all the tension and effort it had taken to be stoic melted away and life would be perfect from now on.

Of course, it wasn't perfect, but it was much improved. I got to see Sophia every day, was promoted to the varsity swim team where I distinguished myself not at all, thrived in my physics and chemistry classes, acquired a boyfriend in time for the Junior Prom, and even hosted successful pool parties.

Eventually, it happened. Mom was assigned to be a substitute teacher in my geometry class. This was not a strong subject for her, but I was surprised when she walked in. She looked serious, formal even, and determined as she introduced herself and took roll. I had never seen her look so professional—gone was the chirpy social banter she usually engaged in. She looked a little nervous when we were going over the Pythagorean theorem to find the hypotenuse of a triangle, but she recovered, and the class behaved. Whew, we got through that one and only one person asked me if we were related.

Mom and Dad dragged me on university visits in Northern California and Oregon, but they were of little interest to me because I didn't much care where I went, as long as it was away from home. There was no talk of going anywhere further afield—the west coast was good enough and state schools were practically free. California State University at Chico became my first choice, mostly based on the small, walkable campus, beautiful Romanesque architecture of the older buildings and the natural setting with Big Chico Creek flowing through campus on its way from Lassen National Park to the Sacramento River.

At Drake, I made the dean's list, aced the language arts part of the SAT and ACT standardized tests, and squeaked through the math portion. Armed with six units of advanced placement credits, I was ready to put my childhood behind me and head to college as an all-American coed. Or something like that.

11

Freedom in Chico

COLLEGE

I n 1975, I was seventeen and ready to take on the world. Everything I ever dreamed of had come true, and I was the new kid in school again—but this time, so was every other freshman on campus." The three-hour drive to Chico from Marin County flew by, even in our anemic Pinto, crammed to the hilt with bedding and luggage.

Two dorms, Shasta and Lassen Halls, were mostly populated with freshmen students, as older students tended to migrate to the off-campus dorms or their own apartments after the first year. The matching low-slung, three-story brick buildings separated men in the Shasta building from women in the Lassen building with a strip of lush, green grass. Big Chico Creek meandered peacefully through the campus behind Lassen Hall. Lined with leafy trees, it was a beautiful, park-like setting on the edge of campus.

When I entered my bare dorm room, it looked sterile and stern with two utilitarian looking desks under the single window, two skinny twin beds along the long walls and two closets at the foot of the beds. I loved it. After claiming my half of the room, Mom and I quickly made the bed with the flowery bedspread she had purchased. The long bulletin board above the bed was quickly covered with David Bowie posters. I put my pens and notebooks in the desk and hung my clothes in the tiny closet, wondering who my roommate would be. We checked out the large, shared bathroom and found the laundry room when we passed a large piano in a community room. "Oh, look, I can still play the piano," I said, with a momentary flush of enthusiasm that was never realized. I never played the piano again. My concert piano potential had never recovered after my disastrous recital in sixth grade.

After Freshman Orientation, Mom shed a tear, Dad gave me a hug, and I felt a brief pang of sadness and a little trepidation as I watched my parents walk away, hand in hand, toward our little chocolate-brown Pinto. I turned toward my new life with outstretched arms, racing across the grass to meet my new roommate, who turned out to be a little strange. She talked constantly about sex, wanting to have sex, dreaming of sex, and plotting how to get sex. I wandered down the hall and found a group who invited me to go out with them. That night, I went to my first off-campus party and stayed out until after midnight, reveling in the freedom to do whatever I wanted. The freedom I had dreamed about for years.

I missed my long talks with Sophia and wished she could have come with me. She might have thought I was prettier, but I knew for sure that she was smarter. I had always envisioned her going off to the fancy university in New York on her scholarship, while the state school in California was good enough for me. The summer after we graduated from high school, she went off the rails, rebelled against her parents, moved in with a tow-truck driver, and never went back to school. Mom and I were horrified, and we tried everything we could think of to get her to change her mind. She wouldn't budge. It disheartened me to think that my friendship, and all the deep conversations and support we had shared, wasn't enough to fill the deep void of doubt she harbored inside.

We drifted apart precipitously, and she wanted nothing to do with my new life. I was disappointed, but for me it was just another move and another set of friends.

SOCIAL LIFE

As an only child who now lived in a group setting, I felt like a kid in a candy store. I could walk out of my room nearly any time of day or night and find people in the halls or with their doors open, ready to socialize.

In the middle of the first semester, I met Cindy, who lived on the same floor in the dorm. We joined forces to go to a frat party.

"What time is it? There's another party we could go to," she said as we stood around sipping beer from red plastic cups. Already a little tipsy, I turned my wrist to check my watch, pouring beer on her foot.

"Oops, sorry," I said. Her hearty laugh broke the awkward moment, and she became the best partner for everything college had to offer, from chasing boys to finding the best parties to scoping out unique classes to fulfill our core requirements. She was vivacious and full of energy, with a mop of honey brown curls, ready to drop everything for a moment of levity.

"Want to go to a party?" she'd ask.

"Sure, I can study later," would be my typical response, always reluctant to pass up a fun time.

"Hey, I found a great class—should be an easy A. Want to take it?"

"Sure. What's electronic music?" The music class was not easy, and I got a C, but it was fun.

"Want to go to a concert this weekend? Wendy's driving."

"Sure, I can write that paper later." She always had something to offer that was more fun than studying or writing papers.

Cindy's loyal friendship provided the anchor I needed to seek adventure and ground me when things spiraled. After some reshuffling of roommates, the overly flirtatious one moved out, and through a random assignment, Kelli moved in. In our second year, Kelli became a Resident Advisor and moved into her own room, while Cindy and I became roommates. Cindy, Kelli, and I joined forces with three other girls, Wendy, Gail, and Sue, cementing bonds that would last a lifetime as we transitioned from naïve seventeen-year-olds to career women armed with university degrees. We survived the shock of our first university report cards, made matching costumes for Halloween, and got fake IDs. The world of rock music, concerts, and bootleg albums came alive as we listened to Led Zeppelin, the Rolling Stones, and Peter Frampton. The smell of pot hung in the air and people disappeared into back rooms, sniffing lines of cocaine. I felt so alive, like everything I used to read about in books was finally happening to me. I was living my life to the fullest, with a wide circle of friends and no pesky parental rules to follow.

We paid little attention to the news, but I caught the occasional newscast on the TV in the common room of the dorm, and Cindy was taking a lot of political science classes. War had broken out in Lebanon, and while I hoped it would be a minor skirmish, images showing the destruction of Beirut devastated me. It was a place that had held so much beauty and comfort for me both times we had been evacuated. Now my place of refuge—the Paris of the East, with the lovely hotel pool and outdoor cafes—was a pile of rubble. I was consoled by Cindy and her poly sci professor, who welcomed students into his home and held forth with his analysis of world events. It was immensely satisfying to have a serious conversation with such a learned man who was so humble. Until he asked me out. My vision shifted, and I doubted my perceptions. Was this his way of getting a date? What a turnoff. It reminded me of the man on the ship, when I thought he was being nice because he was my friend, but it turned out he had other motives. I wasn't going to fall for that.

My boyfriend from high school didn't last three months. Replacements came in a long line of blond, handsome men. The pace of discarding them created a familiar rhythm. Just like our frequent moves, the beginning was fresh and exciting until cracks started showing and fascination with guns, military paraphernalia, and disco dancing didn't feel like such a great fit. One blond man, this one a frisbee player and first to graduate with a diploma in a brand-new major offered at Chico State, computer science, was too drenched in the party lifestyle to last despite his kind and attentive nature. An artist, musician, physics tutor, and basketball player followed—the list rolled on, but it was never the perfect balance of ambition, intellect, and fun.

The endings were often messy. My high school boyfriend, suspecting infidelity, struck me in my face as he was driving us down the highway. I never saw it coming, the blow striking my left cheek. It startled me but didn't hurt and I went numb, retreating into my inner safe place where my energy constricted into my raisin state, like it always did when I was overwhelmed with emotion. I stared straight ahead and didn't say a word as apologies fell from his mouth and dissolved into the floorboard. I felt wooden as we sped down the road, but he had crossed a line. He dropped me at my parent's house, and I never saw or spoke to him again.

With another boyfriend, we got into an argument over a trifling matter and my usual easy-going manner flipped like a pancake, with rage building in me that was out of proportion to the event. He looked shocked and faded away. In another incident, a man I was dating got frustrated, saying, "Why don't you talk? You look like a robot." I felt like a robot. I was completely numb inside. When the argument started, I could feel anger stirring, but then it evaporated and I sat quietly shrinking into myself, feeling like a turtle withdrawing into a hard shell. Becoming smaller and smaller, I waited it out ... whatever "it" would bring. More words, a blow, I didn't know. I was sad and depressed for a few days or weeks after each breakup, but there was always another someone waiting in the wings. The giddiness of a new relationship glossed over the pain with the promise that things would be different.

GRADES

My love of science in high school led me to a microbiology major with many lab classes. I didn't realize that lab sessions were three hours compared to one hour for a regular class yet were for the same number of credits. I was irked that my friends taking business and general education courses seemed to have a lot more free time while I was stuck inside twirling test tubes and firing Bunsen burners.

I developed a series of health problems that landed me in the emergency room several times, including serious allergic reactions and intractable back pain that made it hard to stand at laboratory benches for long periods. The doctors couldn't figure out what I was allergic to, and the recommendation for bed rest for my back meant I missed a great deal of class and lab time.

My Introduction to Psychology and US History classes weren't too demanding, but late nights partying alternating with episodes of intense pain meant that the 8:00 AM History class was often conducted without me. The Principles of Biology class seemed so easy that I skipped some of those lectures, too.

Sitting in a windowless, cell-like study room at the end of the hall a few days before final exams, a place unfamiliar to me, I tried to memorize dates for my history class, quickly realizing that they weren't sticking. Biology was no better when it dawned on me that the class had quickly accelerated from the easy review material I had seen at the beginning. I had waited too long and there was too much to learn. The next day, staring at the blank spaces on my test, my stomach clenched, and I felt sweaty and damp. I knew I was in trouble.

I was distraught to learn that class attendance counted for a big part of the grade—perhaps I missed that information because I didn't attend the first class. First semester grades were crisis time. The A grade in Beginning Ballroom Dance and Psychology didn't begin to balance the horrific D in US History and C in Biology. I had never gotten a D before. And the C in Biology, which was required for my major, should have been a breeze after all the science classes I had in high school. Getting that C was an enormous blow. Mom and Dad were shocked, though I had tried to warn them I had missed a lot because of my health problems. I received my grades over winter break and wondered how everyone else did. It was some consolation when I returned to school in January to learn that most of my friends were as distressed as I was, and one girl didn't even come back. Her grades were so bad, she decided college wasn't for her.

That was a revelation. I hadn't understood that not finishing school was a possibility. I could see my future crumbling, realizing that I couldn't put off studying until finals week ever again. There was another side to this calamity though. Because so many friends did poorly in the first semester, I felt a delicious sense of belonging. I was a part of the bad-grade group, even though it was a blow to the part of me that wanted to succeed.

We all vowed to do better, with study time coming before party time . . . at least during the week. Except Thursday was a big party night on campus, so we couldn't miss that. This left Monday, Tuesday, and Wednesday for intense concentration on school. I made sure to never take another 8:00 AM class and got an A in Government the second semester. However, taking two lab classes meant I had many long hours between lecture and lab for Zoology and Inorganic Chemistry and I focused so much on my baffling chemistry class that I managed to pull a C out of content that made no sense. However, Zoology class suffered, and I wondered if I, like the other girl, wasn't college material.

Mom and Dad were perplexed but tried to help by encouraging me to take fewer classes and get my feet on the ground. There were also a few reprimands from them about studying more and partying less, though they were pleased and relieved that I had a strong social network.

In my sophomore year, I only took four classes instead of five, but my health problems persisted, and my grades were still poor. Medicated on pain pills, I could barely comprehend what was happening to me. I loved school. How could I be so bad at it? I could understand bombing out of the first semester, but most of my friends had pulled it together enough to get decent grades while mine were still in the basement. That wonderful feeling of belonging faded away. I was mad at myself for not trying harder, and my rickety confidence threatened to crumble. Unlike my previous schooling, I couldn't be rescued by being whisked away to another country for a fresh start; I had to figure out a way to make this work.

Cindy was constantly juggling work hours and calculations about how much money she had, as her parents didn't support her education. I watched as she and other friends scrambled to make enough money to pay tuition and support themselves. I started to realize how fortunate I was that my parents covered my basic expenses, and I only had to focus on school. That made my dismal report card performance even more embarrassing.

I never thought I'd need counseling, but I was desperate to turn things around. My parents weren't around, to my relief, but I didn't know where to turn for help. Our Resident Advisor in the dorm suggested student counseling. It turned out to be surprisingly helpful. The counselor helped me work through identifying the things I liked about science (understanding how living things work) and suggested other majors that related to science. Visiting a medical laboratory at Enloe Memorial Hospital, a field trip associated with my microbiology class, was even more clarifying. After looking at rows and rows of white-coated people bent over microscopes, I knew microbiology and laboratory science wasn't a satisfying fit. Connecting with people was what I sought, not being cloistered in a lab for the rest of my life. A major in Health Science and Biology allowed me to consider roles where I could interact more with people than microscopes, perhaps in public health or health education.

Figuring that I had one more chance, I took only three classes in the Spring. The two real classes, Health Science and Bacteriology, both met the requirements for my major. Jogging class was an easy A. The other two received more attention from me than any class ever had. I even devoted some Thursday nights studying, and my report card glowed with a radiant B grade in both of the *real* classes. Jogging was not a mental challenge, but after months of bedrest, it was freeing to move my body. Surprisingly, my back started feeling better with the added exercise and after adding long bike rides through Bidwell Park, I started feeling stronger. What a relief. Finally, I was getting the hang of how to study, and my health issues were resolving. Looking back at my first two years, I realized I hadn't known what it meant to study because I had always picked up new material easily, even with all the moves. I hadn't ever been challenged to learn difficult concepts, and with a lot of time alone at home, I could study at my leisure. The new sense of freedom and having a large group of friends in college was exhilarating, but it took some time for me to learn how to balance study time with social time.

My grades steadily improved, even as I added more course credits to my load, sometimes taking as many as seven classes. Summer school and intercession classes allowed me to make up for the previous light semesters. I was one happy student the first time I made the Dean's List and by the time I graduated, As and Bs littered my report card. Not only that, I made it out in four years.

12

Indonesia Bound

JAKARTA

While I adjusted to university life, Mom and Dad got welcome news that Dad had a new assignment. True to his word, he had accepted no overseas jobs while I was in high school, but now they were eager to resume their expat lifestyle, this time in Indonesia. Dad's boss, Mr. Hsu, who had worked with him in Dacca, had continued mentoring Dad during his time in the home office. Mr. Hsu quickly tapped him as project manager for the Sederhana (which means "simple" in Bahasa Indonesian) Irrigation and Land Development Project, based in Jakarta. It was a sprawling three-way venture between the government of Indonesia, a Taiwan-based consulting firm and the International Engineering Company. The goal was to help small farmers increase their rice production by growing more than one crop per year across the archipelago. As one of Dad's Indonesian colleagues used to say, "Little by little, slowly." It was a good mantra for the collection of small projects spread across almost all of Indonesia's twenty-seven provinces. I was shocked to learn there are more than 6,000 inhabited islands out of the 18,000 in the country. They taught the farmers to build weirs and diversion dams to create small wading pools in the rice paddies and use plants that matured in three or four months instead of six months.

On my visit home during the holidays, I helped pack up a few of our mementos to ship back to Grandma and Grandpa in Texas, including my doll, Chuz, my brass camel collection from Pakistan, and our *huacos* from Peru. Mom and Dad moved to Jakarta in Spring 1976, halfway through my first year of college. They left me with stern instructions to study hard, but it seemed perfunctory. Did that mean they were confident that I'd figure it out? Or were they simply distracted? They seemed uncharacteristically blasé about whether I'd flunk out or not. When school let out and everyone else packed up to scatter across California to their childhood homes to work or play or attend summer school, I boarded a flight to Manila and Singapore before landing in the sultry, tropical heat of Jakarta. I was carrying my fourth US passport. This one was the first with the blue cover, instead of green, that was adopted in the US bicentennial of 1976. My long brown hair was parted in the middle with "Farrah Fawcett" bangs that winged out to the side, a style popularized by the actress in the TV show *Charlie's Angels*.

Thus began the start of the next phase of my double life, split between Chico, a rural college town in Northern California, and Jakarta, a city teeming with six million people. Rice paddies lined the roads around both Chico and Jakarta, but the similarity ended there. Chico's Mediterranean climate, with hot summers and cool, wet winters, supported many almond and walnut orchards beyond the rice fields, while Indonesia was lush and tropical with coffee, rubber, banana, and palm oil plantations.

Going overseas and being in the tropics after four years in Marin County was freeing. I never felt like I fit into suburban life and while college stimulated me, I was most at home when I was on the move. Put me in an airport, and I immediately felt like I belonged, like I was in the right place to be me. The bigger the airport, the better.

Hong Kong, Taipei, Singapore, Jakarta—all of them felt like home with the constant movement, never sleeping, the ebb and flow of passengers heading to the far corners of the world, and best of all, the romantic place names flashing on the board from books I had read or places I wanted to go: Seoul, Kuala Lumpur, Siem Reap, New Delhi, Abu Dhabi, Bombay.

I hunched over the window at the end of the two-hour flight from Singapore, which hung off the end of the Malay Peninsula, to Jakarta, perched on the western edge of Java. As far as I could see, a network of canals cut through masses of low buildings with red tile roofs.

As I stepped off the air-conditioned airplane, the hot, humid air smacked me in the face like a wet washcloth. I inhaled deeply, feeling the heaviness of the damp air. I noticed there were no women in purdah, even though Indonesia was Muslim. It appeared more relaxed than Pakistan or Bangladesh in terms of how women dressed, but there was still the familiar call to prayer five times a day.

Our house was the best we had ever had, with spacious, airy rooms and thick vegetation in the front yard and inner courtyard. We had over thirty banana trees loaded with fruit, along with coconut, papaya, and tapioca trees. "Hello, Bird," I'd call out to Mom's caged mynah bird, rewarding him with banana and papaya from our trees when he squawked. He replied, "Hello, Bird," back to me before he combed his jet-black feathers with his thick, orange beak.

The American Club was slightly shabby, the restaurant and event rooms showing their age, but it was refreshing to cool off in the Olympic-sized pool where I swam endless hours of laps. Both the adults that Mom knew and the kids my age seemed to dislike everything about Indonesia, including the school, weather, and food. About the Indonesians, all I heard was, "They're unfriendly and always try to rip you off." Mom said it was like Pakistan all over again and she had to find friends outside of the club who were more fun. Most of the kids I met were still in high school, so I didn't fit in and couldn't understand why they complained about their gleaming, spacious modern school with a fully stocked gymnasium. All we had had in Dacca was a weed infested single basketball court. The Jakarta International School was better funded than the Dacca American Society School, though I heard that a modern school had opened in Dacca after the war.

The following summer after my sophomore year, I met a whole new group of friends at the American Club who were much more positive and upbeat about everything. It was as if the whole expat community turned over and the new group was positive and welcoming, inviting me to movie nights, parties, and overnight trips to visit other parts of Indonesia.

MOM

Mom seemed to be flourishing into someone I barely recognized, working as a Ganesha docent in the National Museum of Indonesia in Jakarta, an archeological and historical museum. She studied the material she was expected to know, poring over manuscripts of explorers who had encountered rare plants, animals, and primitive stone carvings. She started doing restaurant reviews, wrote travel articles, and was published widely in local newspapers and regional magazines, eventually getting published in the San Francisco *Chronicle* and *Los Angeles Times*. I couldn't understand what had happened to her. Who was this woman and where had she been all these years? One day, it struck me. It was my place in the family that had changed. I wasn't there anymore. That's when I understood Mom had devoted her life to me and put all her desires on hold. I felt guilty and very loved at the same time. I was so proud of her and celebrated every success.

"Mom, if you're so interested in all this stuff, why didn't you major in archeology or geography?" We were sitting with Bird, and Mom was surrounded with old books from the library and museum.

"Anthropology. That's what I would have majored in if I had any idea it existed."

"Why did you major in Home Economics?"

"It was a silly major, but I didn't know any better. I had fun being a majorette at University of Texas—being a baton twirler at the footballs games was a blast. Grandad picked out the major for me, and he just expected me to go to college to find a husband. I showed him. I became a flight attendant when I graduated. That suited me a lot better than baking bread, setting the table properly, and knowing the difference between a fork and finger buffet. Now I have to make up for lost time."

TRAVEL

My first summer in Indonesia, Mom and I established a pattern that we maintained for seven of the ten years my parents were there, traveling around the islands. During those seven years, I was in school and had summers off. Dad was always working, so he couldn't accompany us. However, he got plenty of travel on the job as he cycled through job sites, even visiting places in Borneo and Papua New Guinea, where he had been based in the Navy in World War II.

It was 1976 when Mom and I took our first of many trips to Bali. The dissonant sounds of gamelan percussion orchestras and fragrant clove cigarettes that perfumed the air enchanted us. The airport was the only place on the island with electricity. We made our way to sleepy Kuta Beach where there were a few *losmen* (small, family-run guesthouses), a couple of small open-air cafés and the long sweep of the most gorgeous sandy beach I had ever seen. Our *losmen* was perfectly situated to catch the deep crimson sunsets playing off billowing white cumulous clouds over the Indian Ocean. The fresh sea breeze was scented with jasmine by day and grilled lobster at night. Days and nights were evenly matched, perched as we were right under the equator, and we quickly fell into the rhythm of the island. We rose with the sun and wound down at dusk when the kerosene lamps came out for a couple of hours.

Our breakfast on the front porch of our *losmen* delighted our taste buds with a sweet banana, thick piece of freshly baked bread, and cup of rich, black coffee from the local plantation. A couple of Australian surfers at the shore complained bitterly about how Bali was changing for the worse with so many tourists and would never be the same. There was hardly anyone on the beach and the place was so sleepy that I couldn't imagine that it could be much quieter.

Bali was so different from Java and the rest of Muslim Indonesia because it was Hindu. There were no mosques and no calls to prayer. Daily offerings were left to the deities in the form of small, intricately woven baskets folded from coconut or banana leaves with small bits of rice, fruit, colorful flowers, and a stick of smoldering incense. The Balinese spent hours each day constructing these vibrant symbols of gratitude to the gods, gently placing them in every corner of the island, accompanied by a prayer. They were placed at temples, statues, fountains, doorways, walkways, homes, shops, beaches, motorcycles and every other nook and cranny. The artful offerings perfumed the air with the scent of frangipani and incense.

We loved going to Made's Juice Bar, a rustic shack selling delicious fried rice, mango lassi, and the best *jaffles*—grilled sandwiches made with avocado, crab, cheese, and tomato. We went there nearly every day. The second year, Made's had a proper building and when the kids saw me, they came running out, shouting, "Inga's back, Inga's back," a scene that was repeated annually, even when the kids were teenagers. I was touched that they remembered me. Everyone in the village went to the beach at sunset each evening and we enjoyed turtle skewers, grilled on a tiny hibachi in the sand, and frog's legs fried in butter.

We had the *losmen* to ourselves until a tall, scrawny, redheaded young man moved in. Brandon had a mysterious and pensive air about him. He was soft-spoken and shared only a few things about himself, aside from his origin in Queensland, Australia, and that he had been coming here for years to surf. He didn't think Bali was ruined and said he felt at home here. Mom tried to draw him out, but he was guarded. It surprised me when he offered to take me around the island the next day, but I eagerly accepted. "Don't forget your sunnies," he said. I looked blank. "Sunglasses."

The next day, we mounted a motorcycle rigged to carry a surfboard. Leaving Kuta behind, we traveled south down a deserted road through low vegetation. Brandon pulled over at a barely visible trail and a few bedraggled children materialized, chattering away with him in Bahasa Indonesian. He led the way down the faint goat track with the surfboard, losing the kids when they got bored. I could see water in the distance and suddenly the track petered out, and we were standing atop a giant cliff.

"What is this place?" I was breathless from the walk and the striking beauty of the scene.

"It's called Uluwatu. No one comes here except a few surfers. It's a special place. There's nothing but water from here to Australia."

"It's wonderful." I gazed over a striking stretch of cobalt blue ocean with perfectly spaced waves reaching toward the shore. We were on a small knob of land that jutted out from Bali, like a drop of water that almost got squeezed off but still clung to the rest of the island by a thin thread of land we had crossed. We were at the extreme southern end of the island with the whole Indian Ocean spread before us. The rhythmic sound of the waves formed the backdrop of the hundred-foot scramble down to the beach.

"Remember, I've never surfed before," I said nervously.

"That's OK. You can swim, right?"

'Of course. I was on the swim team."

"You can swim while I surf a little. Just be careful of the reef." I had been around many beaches but only to frolic where the water met the shore. He flung his board down and beckoned me to follow. I tried to stroke through the waves but kept getting pushed back, scraping my knees on the coral as I tumbled like I was in a washing machine. Soon, tiny pinpricks of blood oozed from multiple spots. When I stood in the shallow water, he saw my bloodied legs. Horrified, he apologized profusely for putting me in danger, as he saw how inexperienced I was in these conditions. We went back to the beach. "We'd better get you back so we can clean those cuts, or they'll get infected."

It embarrassed me that I didn't know what to do in the surf and humbled by the realization that by trying to fake it, I put myself in danger. Being a surf groupie was harder than it looked, unless I was going to confine myself to preening on my beach towel.

The next day, in the gentle breakers off Kuta Beach, he showed me how to read the waves and time my kicks to get through the surf. I played around a little on the board. Gradually we grew closer, and the quiet young man got under my skin. He kept taking me to secret places around the island and we finally kissed under a full moon, the gently rustling leaves of a banana tree blending with the gentle sounds of surf. I couldn't imagine life being any more perfect than at that moment.

After I left, we corresponded and the next year I saw him again, still curious about his history. Eventually, his story tumbled out. He had been working on a boat and got busted for smuggling drugs in Singapore, which had notoriously strict rules about drug possession that included the death penalty. They had been lenient, only sending him to prison, but the year he spent in a Singapore jail was anything but easy. He had just gotten out when we met him the year before. That explained his wan appearance. This year he was healthy, tanned, and filled out. Instead of frightening me away, it seemed like a swashbuckling pirate story gone wrong, and I felt protective of him. He was my special connection to a world of international intrigue that was more exciting than my conventional life. This was going beyond *Harriet the Spy* and into Agatha Christie terrain.

Typical of the things we did in his world, we chartered a sailboat to a neighbor island, Nusa Dua, with a group of friends. On the boat, we grilled fresh fish for lunch, and dived in the clear, warm water. When we checked in with the *kepala desa*, the local tribal chief on the island, he invited us to stay in his hut and attend a feast in our honor (which we paid a pittance for after a lengthy, good-natured negotiation). By the third year, the distance between our annual visits took a toll and our conversations felt stilted. He sailed away on a merchant marine boat to Kenya, and I never saw him again.

In 1976, Mom found a slim guidebook with an orange cover, "*Indonesia & Papua New Guinea*," by Bill Dalton. Dalton was a hippie backpacker and acquaintance of both Tony Wheeler, who later founded *Lonely Planet* guidebooks, and Rick Steves, who went on to inspire millions to visit Europe through his guidebooks and other media. Dalton, temporarily based in Australia, found that his little book of narrowly spaced print and roughly edited notes about the Indonesian archipelago was immensely popular.

It was in Sydney that Dalton bumped into Tony Wheeler, where they exchanged tips on inexpensive presses that would print their respective notes on Southeast Asia travel. Dalton went on to found Moon Publications with a series of guidebooks that appealed to a large pool of independent travelers looking for an alternative to *Fodor's* and *Frommer's* luxury guides. Moon Publications and *Lonely Planet* fit Mom's philosophy and style of travel with their humble guesthouse recommendations and insider tips for finding the best hole-in-the wall restaurants. Guidebook in one hand, notes from the museum in the other, she gallivanted across Borneo, Sumatra, Flores, and Irian Jaya, disappearing deeper and deeper into the jungle. Often, we only had the vaguest idea where she was, communications being sketchy.

I again became Mom's traveling companion for excursions that became increasingly less about visiting tourist sites and more about exploring lesser-known spots in search of rare plants or archaeological sites. I was the ideal partner because I was entirely malleable and available for long stretches of time. We traveled by plane, ferry, *bemo* (shared-ride minibus), *becak* (bicycle rickshaw) and foot.

While hunting for the rare rafflesia plant in Meru Betiri National Park on the eastern end of Java, we were taunted by scores of rogue monkeys throwing rocks at us. They were cute at first, but after landing on my shoulders, pulling my hair, and trying to tear the pockets off my dress, I quickly tired of their antics.

On an excursion where we scoured open fields looking for primitive stone carvings Mom had heard about at the museum, we ducked flying stones thrown by a pack of children who had never seen *orang putih* (white people), before being rescued by the *kepala desa*, the village chief who held our passports until we departed. He got the crowd quieted down, but they stood around sullenly staring at us, jostling for space, and making our dinner meal excruciating.

In Sulawesi, known as the orchid island for its unusual shape resembling the flower, we plunged through thick jungle and walked endless miles on narrow paths between rice paddies to track down the burial cliff caves of the local Toraja tribe. I almost gave up hope that they existed. The reward for Mom's persistence came when we stared slack-jawed at the intricately carved effigies of the dead hanging high off cliff faces on balconies like wooden windows into the past. Mom and I were in heaven, easing from the strict mother-daughter relationship to co-conspirators in adventure, and college felt extremely far away.

Another transition was looming as my graduation date grew near. I had to figure out what I was going to be when I grew up. The path from the Health Science degree was less clear than my previous plan of becoming a medical technologist if I had completed the Microbiology degree. Torn between pursuing a career in the US or finding a way to keep traveling the world, I sorted through possible scenarios. I wasn't ready to get married to any of the tall blond men I had dated, didn't know if I wanted kids, and had no desire for a house in the suburbs with a white picket fence. As an only child, I had spent enough time alone and for the first time, realized that I wanted a partner in life. I longed for the right companion. What that meant exactly, I had no idea.

13

A New Beginning in Oakland

NURSING SCHOOL

Ccollege was a time of transition, and I stretched mine out for more than a decade. Once I figured out how to succeed in school, I was like a bee going from flower to flower in search of knowledge. College campuses felt alive with energy and provided an instant community in ways I hadn't experienced in lower grades. I wanted to keep this experience going as long as possible.

After struggling with the decision of what to do after I received my Bachelor of Science degree in Health Science and Biology in 1979, nursing bubbled to the surface. I tested the waters with a summer job as a ward clerk at Enloe Memorial Hospital, which reinforced my interest in health care. I enjoyed science, found myself drawn to helping people, and appreciated the potential for overseas work in a nursing career. That same year, I entered nursing school at the Samuel Merritt Hospital

College of Nursing in Oakland, California, living in a dorm adjacent to the hospital. It was one of the last old-fashioned hospital-based diploma programs because nursing education was moving into the realm of higher education. I chose the program because it provided more hands-on training than university-based curricula.

I was out of sync with my younger classmates, as they were just transitioning from high school, but I loved the culture of hospital life. It felt alive in the same way airports and college campuses made that happen for me; buildings humming with energy twenty-four hours a day. It reminded me of the hospital description in the book, *Cherry Ames: Student Nurse*, that I read in Peru, where she had to walk through eerie underground tunnels. We had the same kinds of tunnels on two levels. The morgue at the hospital where I trained was housed in the creepy lowest tunnel where the light of day never penetrated. Whenever I had to wheel a body down to the morgue with another nurse, we'd whisper as we approached, as if we might disturb a ghost. As soon as we transferred the stiffening body to the refrigerated drawer and the door to the morgue clanged shut, I felt a sense of relief.

Nothing had changed in hospital design or nursing school fashion. Our school was as traditional as Cherry Ames had been, a throwback to the past, still sporting short-sleeved sky-blue shirt dresses with white Peter Pan collars topped with a starched white pinafore, and a long navy-blue cape that resembled the one Cherry wore. Atop our heads we wore huge white folded *Flying Nun* caps, bestowed in a formal capping ceremony. Our nursing instructors added a thin black stripe to a corner of the cap each year, signifying our growing competence.

After the first semester, we could work as student aides. It was terrifying to take on so much responsibility at first, but I knew it would be useful for me to get more hands-on experience after all the book-learning at Chico State. I knew how to learn, but I lacked actual skills. My heart sank when the scheduler assigned me to the oncology unit for my first solo shift without an instructor hovering over me. My supervised clinical shifts for school had been on the orthopedics floor, and I felt comfortable with the many patients recovering from total hip replacements and sports injuries. Cheerful, healthy, and so glad to be relieved of the pain of their worn-out joints, they were in-and-out. Oncology, filled with patients facing death, on difficult chemotherapy regimens and sometimes ineffective drugs for treating side effects, was foreign and intimidating. I survived with a straightforward assignment of patients receiving routine chemotherapy and ended the shift with relief, hoping my next shift would be anywhere else in the hospital. Complaining didn't seem appropriate when they assigned me to oncology again on my second night, but I felt out of my element, unsure of how to talk to patients facing such challenges. Surely the next time I could go somewhere else.

After my third night on the oncology ward, I was hooked, and spent my entire career in that field, seduced by the compassionate team of nurses and doctors, intellectual stimulation of emerging scientific theories, appreciative patients, and my newly discovered capacity to connect to patients facing death, doing so on a deep emotional level without fear. The seasoned nurses on that unit mentored and mothered me for the three years of my training program and then hired me into my first full-time nursing job. Being allergic to the 7 AM day shift start time, I volunteered for evenings and nights. The slower pace and greater autonomy of the late shifts sometimes left me with time to spend with patients, especially with those in pain or fearful during the long, dark nights. I tried to make them comfortable and enjoyed their stories as they went through a mental inventory of their lives.

I experienced my first patient's death one night at two a.m. The end of her life was imminent, and I darted into her room frequently, taking her cool, dry hands in mine and giving them a little squeeze to let her know I was by her side. I wanted her to know she wasn't alone. After wiping her face with a warm washcloth, I gently smoothed her gossamer thin white hair, and applied balm to her chapped lips. Gauze pads, sponge toothbrushes, tubes of petroleum jelly and other assorted medical equipment was scattered across her overbed and bedside tables, so I tidied the room and straightened her sheet, wanting it to look neat if a family member appeared. When I could grab a few minutes in between giving other patients their pain pills or helping them with a bedpan, I sat with the dying patient and watched her thin chest rise and fall like shallow bellows, holding my own breath during the lengthy pauses between breaths. When the pause was exceptionally long one time, I squeezed her hand, but it never rose again. She was gone. I stood in the darkened room with her and wondered what happened between the moment when her features were pliant and animated with the faint breath of life and when she slid to the other side, inert and wooden. It happened in a flash, as if her spirit evaporated in a wisp of faint smoke, leaving the heavy, useless body behind. I treasured this moment and accepted the honor of being with her at the most intimate and vulnerable moment of her life.

OAKLAND FRIENDS

The Chico girls scattered to various graduate degree and training programs, and I acquired a fresh friend group through an acquaintance in Oakland. These new friends, who were several years older than I, differed from anyone I had known before. Alums of the University of California at Berkeley, they discoursed at length on meaty topics such as philosophy and social justice, and created poetry and art. They also did a lot of drugs and lived in communal settings in gritty, urban neighborhoods in Oakland. They were supportive of me, laughing at my endless stream of hospital stories and listening attentively to my Indonesia anecdotes. As I drank it all in, invigorated by being accepted into a bohemian lifestyle I had only read about, my life separated into two tracks.

On one track, I lost myself in the world of dive bars, an abundance of live music, late nights that slid into the soft light of morning, and the harsh underbelly of urban life where a Black Panther was sheltered for a time. Along the way, I dated a musician and gained a new set of club clothing composed of gold boots, patterned pants, and a snazzy fitted jacket. After things fizzled out with the singer, I dated several other men in the group, an older student who turned out to be married, a professor at the college, a doctor at the hospital who also turned out to be married, and a few others. I wasn't terribly discerning because everyone seemed so interesting, most were kind, and I didn't bother to notice clues they weren't emotionally available. Or maybe it was I who wasn't emotionally ready. I certainly lacked a moral compass. Maybe because I had had so many superficial friendships as I transitioned from one country to another and one school to another it seemed easy to cycle through relationships without consequences.

On the other track, I did well in school, and reported for clinical and work shifts on time, if a little sleepy. I stepped from one life into another when I swapped my gold boots for the prim white pinafore, sturdy white shoes, and jumbo-sized white cap of my uniform. I graduated with excellent grades and was hired onto the oncology floor as a fully-fledged registered nurse on the night shift. Was I an adult yet? I didn't feel like one.

Within a few months of graduation, I felt comfortable in my role and set the wheels in motion for the next step: getting a job overseas. I unpacked my manual typewriter, composed letters to Project Hope, the Peace Corps, and the King Faisal Specialist Hospital in Riyadh, Saudi Arabia, which had just opened an oncology unit and advertised for nurses relentlessly in my nursing journals. I mentally packed my bags and waited for positive responses. All three wrote kind and encouraging letters with the same message: get three to five years of experience and we'll be happy to talk to you. That was a setback, so I settled in and contemplated getting another degree while I obtained the required work experience. I would have to settle for travel on the side.

14

Adventures in Asia

A group of three of my closest friends in Oakland were so intrigued with my stories of summers in Indonesia that they wanted to experience them, too. Though I had flown from San Francisco to Jakarta many times by myself, it was my first time leading a group on a multi-stop trip. Mom helped me plan the itinerary through Taipei, Singapore, Java, Bali, and Sydney.

My fifth passport, issued in 1981, was blue, like the previous one, but shrunk to compact size, nearly fitting into the palm of my hand. This one displayed my photograph with my new, short-short haircut. Inspired by the punk rock trend with sharp lines, there was nothing romantic or soft about it. It was an act of rebellion, not wanting to look feminine with long soft waves, especially when I spiked it up for concerts. I didn't think about how it was like Mom's when it wasn't spiky until people said how much we looked alike. When younger, I had always been told I looked like my father, so this was a baffling change in my identity. The last thing

I wanted when I was trying to find myself was to be told I looked like my mother. So much for individuating.

I had always been the follower in the group, but now I was thrust into a different role as the organizer. Our group was comprised of Elise, who was always the life of the party, Julia, who worked in a bookstore and wrote poetry that plumbed the depth of her soul, and Josh, a school psychologist, who was the most dependable of the group. Although they were experienced travelers, they had never been to Asia, and their enthusiasm was infectious. This was going to be easy.

TAIWAN

In Taipei, Julia, Elise, Josh, and I squeezed into one room at the hotel to save money, which flummoxed the staff.

"I'm so sorry. We have a reservation for just one room, but you need more. We will see what we can arrange," said the clerk in accented English.

"No, that's ok. We'll take one room," I said breezily, determined to limit our spending, as this hotel was more expensive than the hostels we planned to stay in for the rest of the trip.

"Oh, but . . ." she said, trailing off like a wave that petered out in the sand, leaving nothing but tiny bubbles, either unsure what to say or how to say it.

"How many beds are there?" asked Josh.

"Two double beds."

"That's fine," he said.

"But . . . " her eyes slid across our faces, presumably trying to imagine how we would get paired up in the beds. We stared back with big smiles. "Please wait." She disappeared into the back room to confer with the other staff, finally emerging to hand us a single key. Was that a disapproving look? Too late, I grasped that our sleeping arrangement was inappropriate, even though the staff wouldn't know it was I who was paired with Josh. Would my parents find out? Would it bring shame to my father? His Taiwanese co-worker had helped with the arrangements.

Oh, no, I thought, *there might be gossip between the driver and the hotel staff and that could get back to the company.* I couldn't figure out how to reverse the situation, so I cringed and went along with it, wishing I had thought this through a little better. We quickly turned toward the elevator.

My father's project involved a consulting firm in Taipei, and they were kind enough to send a driver to pick us up at the airport and tour us around the next day. We got up early to wait in the lobby to minimize any gossip time between the driver and the hotel staff. Everyone in our group was subdued with jet lag as we stepped out under hazy, gray skies to confront the thrum of dense traffic. We came prepared with a list of sights we wanted to see, but the driver had his own agenda.

"Could we do something outside where we could walk around? That might help us adjust to the time change. We have a few ideas." I pointed at my list.

"I think it's better if you go to the National Palace Museum," he said.

"That sounds nice. Can we go to a park first and then to the museum?"

"I suggest you go to the museum first. It is very beautiful." He was exceedingly polite, but I got the impression he was as immovable as a granite pillar.

Stymied, we gathered that the itinerary was out of our hands, so we piled into the car to visit the museum.

I stumbled through the halls with eyes blurry from fatigue, slowly apprehending the importance of this museum. The enormous volume and significance of the collection of antiquities overwhelmed me. There were so many items, but these were only a fraction of the 700,000 items taken from the National Palace in Beijing, China and moved to Taiwan following a series of conflicts with Japan from 1931 to 1949. We were enthralled by the intricate jade carvings, metal works, ceramics, and paintings, and fascinated by the intricate journey these pieces had taken from the Forbidden City to Shanghai, Nanking, Anshun, and Leshan before arriving in Taipei. Our driver beamed with satisfaction when we gushed our thanks, happy that he had accomplished his goal.

SINGAPORE

Singapore presented some unexpected challenges. I'm always slow to recover from jet lag, but others in our group bounced back quickly. We were on our own now, with no driver to shepherd us around. After selecting a hostel from the *Lonely Planet* guidebook, I rejected it right away when the taxi pulled up, seeing that it was amid a chaotic party scene of backpacker hostels and crowds of milling tourists and dissonant disco music. We exited the taxi, but I asked the driver to stay for a minute.

"Let's try another one." I read the next name on the list and directed the driver to take us there.

"What's wrong with this one? This looks like fun," Elise said. The others nodded in agreement.

"You must be kidding. We'll get no sleep." I turned toward the taxi, ready to get back in.

"Who needs sleep? We'll sleep when we get to your parents' house. I'm ready to party." Elise's eyes glowed with excitement. "I know just what I'm going to wear. Let's go." She started walking toward the entrance of the hostel, smiling, and batting her eyes at the assemblage of young, tanned hippie backpackers with long hair, some with tattered bellbottoms, others with loose-fitting harem pants and pukka shell necklaces. I trailed along.

I experienced my first lesson in traveling with others: everyone gets a say, and I wasn't in charge. The group had been polite and demure in Taipei, but they were ready to cut loose now. Elise pulled a fire-engine red jumpsuit out of her knapsack, shook out the wrinkles and performed some magic with the tiny cat's cradle strings that crisscrossed her naked back to keep it loosely in place. Off she went, in search of trouble, staying out until the thin rays of first light peeped over the horizon. From then on, keeping Elise in line proved impossible. She had met one backpacker who seized her quixotic imagination, and we could hardly keep track of where she was off to next, seemingly oblivious to any of the potential dangers I worried about—that she might be drugged, raped, or murdered or who knows what. Was this what Mom worried about when I traveled without her? I felt responsible for the group, at least to get them as far as my parents' house in Jakarta. Josh, who had known Elise much longer than I, pointed out that I had to let go. Besides, Elise sparkled with such enthusiasm I couldn't stay mad at her. She was so vivacious in her red outfit that she mesmerized me as much as everyone else. She shared extended kisses with her paramour, nearly missing the flight to Jakarta, and I breathed a deep sigh of relief when she boarded the plane, half her belongings falling out of her bag as she dragged it down the aisle.

RETURN TO JAKARTA

My parents loved the energy we brought to the house, and we spent many long hours in the garden with Bird, Mom's mynah bird, who squawked and shook his feathers until someone gave him a banana from the tree. Mom probed the depths of Elise's and Julia's entire lives, and they responded with intensely personal stories that I had never heard before. I was startled to hear how Mom, Elise, and Julia conversed like peers instead of the formal tone my younger pals used with my parents when I was in high school and college.

"Do you have any American friends?" asked Elise.

Mom scowled. "I have a few, but expats from other countries are more fun."

"Why is that?"

"The American women complain too much, and most of them just seem to want to go home. They like to stay in the American bubble, going to American Clubs, buying American food from the commissary, and socializing together. I enjoy learning about other customs and perspectives. I get that from my Indian, Malaysian, and Iranian friends at the International Women's Club and the volunteers I work with at Ganesha Society at the museum."

"Who do you travel with when you're exploring the islands?"

"My husband is always working and most of the women don't feel comfortable traveling without men, so I go alone."

"Wow, you're brave." Elise smiled, and Bird ruffled his feathers in agreement. I could see the gears turning in Elise's mind, sensing she could picture herself in this role of the adventurous female traveler casting off societal conventions.

"I like to get out and see village life, listen to gamelan music, and hike through the rice paddies. No one wants to go where I want to go, like to Sumatra and Irian Jaya. They're afraid of the stories they've heard—headhunters and all. But that's probably in the past."

"Headhunters?" whispered Julia.

"*Probably* in the past?" Elise squeaked, her brown eyes wide. Bird responded in kind, delighted to hear bird sounds.

"Probably," Mom said.

"Were you always this adventurous?" asked Julia.

"No, but I was always a little different from most American women. I've liked all the overseas posts we've had, whereas some of the women seem to be biding their time until they can get home. With each new place, I've been able to spread my wings a little more, especially here, when I don't have to worry about keeping Inga safe." She winked at me.

"I want to be like you. Fearless. You should write about travels," said Julia. Elise nodded vehemently in agreement, taking a drag of her clove cigarette.

"I've started writing. I never thought I could get anything published, but the *Jakarta Times* and *Nature Magazine*, another local publication, have been publishing my stories. Now it makes me wonder why I didn't start earlier." Both Elise and Julia looked at Mom admiringly. I did too. I wasn't used to hearing her talk this way, sharing her innermost thoughts, and sounding vulnerable.

This was going well, and I resolved to keep the group on track from now on. Except that Elise kept trying to arrange complicated telephone rendezvous with her beau. This involved our driver or a taxi transporting her downtown to an international call center. When the call came in, her name was announced and she disappeared into an airless booth, closed the door, and tried to devise a plan to meet. I could hear her say, "This woman we're staying with—she travels by herself. I could do that, too.

I could meet you anywhere. Just name the place." Our daily activities revolved around Elise's call schedule and the ever-changing schemes for how she and her paramour were going to connect, but he was hard to pin down.

EAST JAVA

The next leg took us to Jogjakarta by air on Garuda Airlines. We enjoyed touring the Prambanan Complex of Hindu temples by horse and buggy in the late afternoon following a cooling rain. The massive ninth-century Borobudur Buddhist temple, which should have been more notable since it's the largest in the world, impressed us less. The wilting heat and the crush of tourists in the limited public spaces influenced our outlook since most of the complex was off-limits because of the reconstruction work.

Frazzled by the crush of traffic and cacophony of honking horns, we retreated to our modest lodging with a cold Bintang Beer and the *Lonely Planet* guidebook to plot our course.

This hotel provided the others with their first exposure to the Indonesian *mandi*, a practical bathroom design that takes some getting used to. A small, tiled tub filled with water sat next to a ceramic squat toilet that works better than a western toilet if there is low water pressure. Instead of a mechanical flush, water is dipped from the tub using a small plastic dipper.

"The tub seems kind of small. How do we fit in it?" Julia asked.

"I could fit in it," said Elise. They looked at me doubtfully as we stood around the *mandi*.

"You don't get in it. It holds clean water only, so try not to get soap or shampoo in it. Take the dipper and pour water over your body, soap up, pour water again and let it run down the drain. See how the entire bathroom is tiled? It's ok if water gets everywhere. It's cold water, but when it's hot out, believe me, it's refreshing." After our sweaty day at the Borobudur, they agreed that a *mandi* bath was invigorating.

Eager for a change of pace, we made plans to visit Mt. Bromo, an active volcano at the eastern end of Java, the perfect antidote to city life. Third-class tickets didn't get us an assigned seat or even a seat at all. Pressed against a divider with a wicker basket of chickens pecking my legs, I tried to balance myself against a burlap sack of grain. As the wheels clacked along the rail, the heat and general misery rose. I tried to settle into a Zen state to ease my fatigue, but the discomfort was real. Suddenly, there was a commotion near the door. Was that Elise? Was she fainting? I was wedged in so tightly that I couldn't move. I saw her swoon with one hand fluttering over her brow as she slumped against Julia. With much chattering and gesticulating, the Indonesians pushed and prodded others out of seats to make way for her. "*Sakit, sakit, wanita itu sakit.*" I kept hearing, "The woman is sick." I struggled to get over to her, but she saw me coming and gave me a wink. Oh, no, was she faking it? She was. It was all a ruse to get a seat. Her impudence appalled me, but how could I not admire her ingenuity? She was way out of my league. As usual, she charmed and vexed me at the same time. Mostly, I was miserably uncomfortable and didn't think the passengers would fall for a second American tourist getting sick and needing a seat. The heat was nearly unbearable. Attempting to perch on the armrest of a seat, I smiled hopefully at the seated passenger, hoping they wouldn't push me off. After some hours, or maybe it was days, the armrest cut into my leg and time warped. I did what I often did in prolonged uncomfortable situations, such as endless sessions in the dental chair or interminable train rides—I thought about the endless line of refugees in Bangladesh who walked on bare feet into a hopeless future, their villages burned, family members murdered, uncertain where their next meal would come from, and considered how soft and cushy my life was. Even here, no one else looked as bad as I felt; they were used to this. It was I, accustomed to air conditioning, plush seats, abundant food, and pure water, who was different. Surely, I could balance, without complaining, on an armrest on a conveyance that efficiently moved me across the country. When the train stopped, which it did frequently, no one budged from the seats. More people piled in. Sweat dripped down my legs in rivulets. Finally, when I thought I might pass out, a man gently tapped my shoulder and ushered me into the seat he vacated. Grateful beyond words for this precious gift, I could only murmur my thanks, "*Terima kasih, terima kasih.*"

Rousing myself at the train station in Surabaya, we stepped off the train into a confusing welter of *becak, bemo* minibuses, and *becak* bicycle rickshaw drivers all vying for a fare. One man tried to maneuver me into a *becak* while a *bemo* driver pushed Elise into his vehicle nearby. We both jumped out and somehow all ended up in the same vehicle while arguing about where to go. It didn't matter because, even though Elise insisted she gave the driver the name of a *losmen,* he decided we needed to go the Hyatt Hotel, which would have cost three times more than we were planning. Disgusted, I glared at Elise, convinced that she had given him an unintelligible name. I gave the driver the name of the place I had picked out of the guidebook and that was that. I retreated to my solo room to recover while the rest, who had been sitting comfortably for most of the trip and were full of energy, set off for the People's Amusement Park.

Stewing in my room, I considered how I was a chameleon, adapting to their freewheeling lifestyle back home in Oakland, observing, analyzing, and trying to fit in. I wanted to introduce them to *my* lifestyle, but they didn't reciprocate in the same way, unwilling to let me take the lead and sticking with their usual partying routine. I was stuck between two worlds, trying to navigate my imagined role as the experienced Asia traveler, following Mom's precedent, while Elise went off in her red jumpsuit, Josh did what he wanted, and Julia tried to keep the peace.

By the time they came back, bubbling over with excitement at the prospect of a performance of the Ramayana at the park that night, I had recovered. Ready to move on, I buried my feelings as we feasted on *nasi goreng* rice topped with a fried egg, and whole grilled fish, with fried bananas for dessert. The shadow puppet performance of the Ramayana, where the age-old tales of good versus evil played out, delighted us. The puppeteers cleverly manipulated handcrafted leather puppets against a light to cast shadowy figures on a white sheet. Unused to seeing tourists, a friendly mob descended upon us, and Elise nearly stole the show with her red jumpsuit. We all laughed a lot, pretending we could understand the show and their jokes.

The next morning, after another confusing scene at the bus station where I was physically manhandled onto the bus to Probolinggo, as were the others, we found seats, never mind that we were now part of a group of seven in five seats. The bus was fast, the driver faster, and the six-hour drive turned into four. Indonesian transit drivers, desperate for our fare, practically dragged us off the bus, jostling, pushing bodies and pulling arms to maneuver us into a Colt diesel minibus filled with chickens, crates of eggs, sacks of coffee beans, and car batteries.

In Ngadisari, we stayed put for the night and planned to tackle Mt Bromo the next day, like all the other westerners in the *losmen*. Our four double beds might have been placed before the walls were built as they created a continuous mattress with no space for standing or luggage, but by then, we didn't care.

From the other tourists, we learned that the best strategy was to turn in early, then get up in the middle of the night and ride horses to the volcano, preferably with some libations to stave off the cold and expected rain. After procuring some Johnnie Walker Red whiskey for the morning to warm us up, we felt prepared for the adventure. On our way to bed, one of our new friends called out from the open door of their room, which was only slightly larger than our cell.

"Time for a nightcap?" I was over my crabby spell and was ready for some fun, so we all sipped their whiskey from paper cups until it was gone.

"Too bad, that's the last drop," said Evan, tipping the bottle into his mouth.

"We have some in our room," I volunteered.

"What are you waiting for?" I went to get our bottle while Joel went to buy another bottle for the morning. The whiskey was even better mixed with our long-life mocha milk from a waxed paper box and soon, it was midnight. The four beds were spinning, and it was for the best that we were hemmed in by the walls.

The 3:00 AM knock on our door was not welcomed, nor was the patter of raindrops on the corrugated metal roof, but by 3:30 we were mounted on horses, plodding slowly up the cobblestone path. Soaked to the skin within minutes, we stopped by a hotel with bright lights, blaring rock and roll music, and a crowd of people eating rice, noodles, and skewers of grilled *sate*. It looked like an après-ski lodge in full swing. We pulled out the morning ration of Johnnie Walker Red, which had slightly less appeal than the night before, tucked into a bowl of rice, and dried out. Soon we were back in the rain, our guides pointing to where we had just come from down the hill, but we weren't ready to give up, not after going this far.

Insisting on our quest, we prodded the guide to keep going up with his flashlight lighting the trail through the dark night. Suddenly, we were going over the lip of a giant crater, dipping down to the Sea of (soggy) Sands when the first faint shadowy light of sunrise muffled by clouds illuminated an ethereal scene straight out of Star Wars. Our lonely, bedraggled procession dismounted at the base of a cinder cone where we confronted 100 steps. I was gasping even before we reached the crest at the top of the steps. The rain eased up, but my legs quivered from lack of sleep, excessive alcohol, and disused muscles pressed into action. The scene before us was priceless. Steep striated sides of the cone fell away to a cauldron of sulfurous steam that belched like a steam engine rumbling through the center of the earth. It was all worth it—the endless train ride, jouncing bus, tensions with Elise, never ending compromises— none of it mattered in this moment when we could witness this portal into a birth canal of our planet. We embraced, and all was forgiven.

BALI

Still basking in the afterglow of mystical Mt. Bromo, we caught a ferry over to Bali. The difficult overland part of the journey was over and now I was in familiar territory, full of confidence that the group would love this island with its exuberant art, dance, music, colorful flowers, and scents of jasmine, coconut, and clove cigarette. From the landing at Gilimanuk, we caught a *bemo* minibus to Singaraja on the north end of Bali. Being practically unknown to most tourists, there were only a few *losmen*. Following the routine laid down by Mom, I focused on securing a bed before it got too late, but Elise and the others were intent on procuring beer, stopping at the first bar they found. The magic of Mt. Bromo dissipated.

The open-air bar was inviting and when we debated whether to stop or move on, an Australian couple, Megan and Dean, invited us to join them. They ordered Bintang Beer while I inquired about rooms. Sadly, the rooms were full. When they ordered a second round, I wandered out to the road to see if I could see any other *losmen*, but it looked empty. The proprietor gave me directions to another *losmen*, but I couldn't interest Josh or the others in walking there to see if they had a room. Giving up, I decided that we'd do it Elise's way. Afternoon shaded into evening, a spicy dinner of *nasi goreng* and crispy shrimp chips was washed down with more beer. At last, there were yawns.

"Where are you staying?" asked Megan.

"Oh, we don't have a place yet. I guess we'd better think about what we're going to do," said Elise. I didn't say a word.

"But it's so late. Where will you go? There aren't that many places up here," Dean said.

"I don't know; I guess we'll find something," said Elise, laughing and flicking her wavy hair out of her eyes.

I drifted into a reverie, not following the conversation about beds and rooms and plans, until Elise said, "That sounds great. Come on, guys, we have a place to stay."

I stirred, happy to see that Elise's plan worked out after all. Perhaps I needed to loosen up and not worry about things like getting a room before dark. Megan led us to a room with three single beds lined up in a row with just enough room to walk between them and said, "See, three beds. Three couples." She laughed. Elise laughed. I didn't laugh.

I looked at Josh. "Really? We're going to spend the entire night squeezed together on that bed? It's so skinny." It was three inches narrower than a single bed back home.

"Well, come on. Do you have a better idea?" Josh asked.

"I did have a better idea, about six hours ago."

"Why didn't you say anything?"

I stared at him. "You must be kidding. Do you remember when I got the directions to find a place, but no one wanted to go with me?"

"Why didn't you go by yourself?" he said. That was an excellent question.

The six of us took turns brushing our teeth in the tiny *mandi* bathroom, then each pair arranged themselves on the bony beds. Elise and Julia went head-to-toe, while the Australian couple went head-to-head, as did Josh and I. Clinging to the edge of the bed all night, feeling the metal coils digging into my hip, the resonant snores bounced off me. I thought about why I hadn't gone by myself to find a place. I felt responsible for them, but they didn't feel responsible for me. I hadn't wanted to go by myself. Why not? Turning it over again and again in my mind, I muddled through to the answer. Confidence. That was the problem. Lacking the confidence to strike out on my own when the others didn't want to follow, I became a victim. No more. I had a new plan.

At first light, I was off the bed of nails and into the garden for my coffee and toast with a fresh banana, enjoying the quiet of the cool, dewy morning. I asked again about lodging in the area and found out about another place. When the others were up, I gave them a copy of my notes and announced that everyone could find their own lodging for the night. They looked surprised but were pleased when I told them they had become seasoned Indonesia travelers and that I'd help them if needed. While they had breakfast, I walked by myself to the *losmen* down the lane across the highway and found a large, airy room for myself. I enjoyed a relaxing day washing my clothes in the sink, writing in my journal, and reading, a welcome respite from the arduous travel of the past two weeks. We gathered for dinner at the restaurant where we had

had drinks the night before and made plans to go to Kuta Beach the next day and settle in there for a few days. Everyone was happy, especially me.

Soon after I introduced the group to the joys of Kuta Beach, Josh had to get back to work at the school district in Oakland, and Elise was still trying to rendezvous with her erstwhile boyfriend from Singapore. Julia and I wrapped up the last leg of the trip to Sydney, Australia holed up in a sordid hotel room equipped with our only requirements: a tiny TV that beamed Princess Diana's wedding to Prince Charles and a six-pack of beer.

BACK TO THE U.S.

Back in Oakland, working the night shift from 11 PM to 7 AM left me chronically sleep deprived, and I always craved more rest. Slivers of daylight slipped between my blackout window shades, stalling my efforts to sleep. Through my hazy awake hours in my apartment was a running calculation of how much sleep I had banked, and how much I could squeeze in before the next shift. By the time I finished my first year as an RN, I was ready for a change. Enough of the black nights. Enough of the partying on days off. Enough inappropriate relationships. I wanted to be around people who had professional goals and lived active, healthy lives. For the first time, I was making decent money but never had a moment to spend any of it since I slept through daylight hours. I had been coasting through the last year, but being financially independent and becoming more confident gave me the freedom to make new choices. I just wasn't sure what I wanted.

15

Finding Myself

OAKLAND

Sitting in my pale-yellow VW Beetle late one night in Oakland, heart thumping, I tried to stay calm so I could think. The stocky, dark-skinned man with a short afro in the car next to me gestured for me to roll down the window. Grasping the handle, I rolled it down three inches. He gestured to roll it down more. I shook my head. I had been driving home from a nightclub at two a.m. when the car cut me off, then backed up, still angled so I couldn't pass.

"Give me your money," he said tersely. I had my slim club purse with nothing in it but my ID, forty dollars in cash, and a tube of lipstick. I passed it through the open slit and dropped it. He caught it and spent a few moments going through it.

"My friend here wants you to get out of the car." A mental reel of the story of a friend who had been kidnapped by a group of men and raped flashed through my mind like a movie at ten times the normal speed. The only reason she had escaped was because the car they were driving was pulled over for a missing taillight.

"No. I gave you my money. That's all."

"He really wants you to come with us."

I shook my head. No way, not going to happen. I wouldn't open the locked door. There was more discussion in their car that I couldn't hear. I saw the glint of a firearm. My thumping heart threatened to burst from my chest. I squinted at the narrow space ahead of me. Could I get through? It was tight. I had to take a chance. I eased the clutch, slid the stick shift into first gear. Shooting forward, the engine whined. Shoulders tense, I made it through the gap. Pressed as hard as I could on the accelerator. I heard their car behind me. I waited for the gunshot. Whipping the steering wheel to the right at the corner, I headed toward MacArthur Boulevard, a busy, well-lit, multilane street. Racing down the boulevard, I glanced in the rear-view mirror. They were gone. For the first time, I appreciated the souped-up engine the previous owner had installed. Shaking, I drove to the communal house of friends who calmed my hysteria, then returned home without even thinking of calling the police. This was life in the big city. Nothing unusual, I thought. Never-ending stories of violent incidents among friends and colleagues surrounded me.

We did the best we could to stay safe, support each other, and shield ourselves in emotional armor against a world of anarchy. This was urban living, vibrant, even with the warts. Armed with a sense of invincibility, I never considered safety to be an issue.

After this incident, and with my new feeling of confidence and financial freedom after the Indonesia trip, I was ready for a move. My best friend, Cindy, returned from her graduate program in Arizona, providing just the excuse I needed for a change of lifestyle.

SAN FRANCISCO

Cindy and I moved into an apartment in the desirable Cow Hollow neighborhood in San Francisco where I could walk to my new job on the oncology unit at California Pacific Medical Center. This position offered more opportunities for advancement, and I thought it was time to put some distance between me and the hedonistic existence I had been living. I was still on night shift but with a twist. It was a day-night rotation, with a switch every two weeks. While tough on my circadian rhythm, being on the day shift allowed me to gain more experience administering complex chemotherapy regimens, collaborating with physicians, and participating in special projects.

San Francisco was only about ten miles from Oakland, but it was a world away. In Oakland, I had adapted to constant intrusions into my personal space, ranging from repeated car break-ins to an apartment burglary and a late night hold up. After the move, I slowly relaxed, realizing that "city" didn't equal "violence", at least to the same degree, letting my situational awareness drop a couple of notches. I felt safer in the most remote corners of San Francisco than I ever did in Oakland.

Oakland was a hyper-urban mix of Blacks and Whites in a gritty city with tangy BBQ, fried chicken and waffles, surrounded by violence and a tenacious survival attitude paired with a strong sense of community. In San Francisco, I worked with a mix of Whites and a mélange of Asian co-workers including Filipino, Chinese, Korean, Japanese, Indian, Laotian, and Hmong with more courtesy and potlucks brimming with chicken adobo, sushi, and potstickers, but less frank talk and close ties.

In San Francisco during my night shift rotations, I welcomed every sunrise, signaling the end of my shift as the first golden rays tickled the top of the sharp end of the Transamerica pyramid and the tubular tip of Coit Tower. Working on the 6th floor of the hospital campus at the top of Pacific Heights afforded million-dollar views of the Golden Gate Bridge and San Francisco Bay. I never took the beauty and softness of that first light over the gentle city for granted, filling my soul with gratitude and peace.

Kim and Elizabeth, also new hires on the oncology unit, were my age and full of exuberant energy, intellectual curiosity, and caring nursing styles. We bonded instantly. They drew me like a magnet to their deep souls. Kim, whose "y'alls" and hint of Texas twang gave away her origins and exuded joy and relentless positivity, drawing people in and never letting them go. Elizabeth's quick wit and good humor gave way occasionally to angst-ridden depths that added to her intensity and allure. Tall and vibrant, we turned heads when we dressed up to go out on the town, Kim radiant with her long, thick red hair, and pale skin, Elizabeth, and I with similar brunette pixie-bob haircuts. Elizabeth and I looked alike enough that doctors and patients often mixed us up. More than once, a puzzled patient asked why I had changed clothes in the middle of my shift.

Eliane, with her dark hair, fine features, and flashing eyes, and Laureen, who batted her eyes and tossed her blonde locks, along with endless quips, joined other young, newly minted nurses in the oncology unit.

Dr. Duncan stood before the large whiteboard in front of the nurse's station, staring at the assignments, shaking his head.

"Is something wrong?" I asked.

"What's with these names? All these new nurses and I can't keep them all straight. What's wrong with Smith and Jones?" he said in a teasing tone, pointing at the whiteboard names Eliane Apheceix and Inga Aksamit.

"It's not so hard. Here, I'll help you out. Mine is In-gah Ak-sa-mit, and this is Elly-on Af-eh-sex. Elizabeth Kassay isn't so hard, but we look alike, so that can be confusing. And look, Kim Hudson, nothing hard about that one, and she's easy to remember because she's the only one with red hair." It reminded me of so many first days of school, and, like my teachers, he eventually got to know each of us.

Our friend group expanded, eventually blurring with the Chico group cycling into San Francisco with new entry-level jobs in the professional ranks. We dated medical interns and residents, ordered expensive drinks at the grand St. Francis Hotel, made the rounds of the latest restaurant openings, and followed up-and-coming bands. My new urbane persona included season tickets to the ballet, attendance at the high-society Black and White Ball, and two luxurious silk dresses that rotated through many events. I was sampling different lifestyles like new clothes, trying them on for size.

Eliane talked me into renting a cabin in Tahoe to feed our passion for skiing. We recruited other nurses and doctors to share the rent. The Tahoe ski resorts were only three hours from San Francisco and ski leases running from November to June were common. Since the nurses had to work every other weekend and had random days off during the week, and the doctors-in-training had irregular shifts, some weeks the cabin was occupied every night but never were we all there at once. Most of the cabins were built decades before and the décor tilted toward avocado green kitchen appliances, dark wood cabinets, and burnt orange carpets. All we wanted was a bed and access to the mountains.

Our overseas assignments in tropical latitudes had provided little opportunity to experience snow when I was a child. Having only skied twice, I could barely do a snowplow when I joined the group cabin, but I loved the sensation of sliding across the snow in crisp, fresh air. Wanting to get better as fast as possible, I spent nearly every day off driving up to the mountains in winter. Sometimes we'd ski all day. Eliane would drive us back to San Francisco, and I'd try to nap in the car before she'd drop me off at 11 PM for my night shift.

Eliane was on a mission to become an expert skier, and her next move was to sign us up for a week-long advanced ski camp at Squaw Valley, the site of the 1960 Olympics that was known for its steep slopes. It was clear that "advanced" was a stretch for me. The ski coaches assigned Eliane to the highest skill group, and I wondered how many years it would take before I could catch up to her. We were exhausted at the end of every day, doing drills, skiing the steeps, and learning how to race through slalom and giant-slalom gates. By the second year, when we signed up again, we were both in the most advanced group. Part of the reason I got better so fast was because I was dating Judd, our tall, blond ski coach, and I got non-stop coaching when I skied with him.

"Point your skis over the edge, drop off, knees bent," said Judd. "And don't forget to breathe." I hovered at the edge, every muscle tensed, my mind already flying off the small drop. But my body said NO. Muscles stayed tense and the longer I stood frozen, the harder it was to go. I slid forward a hair, fear in my throat. Gravity took over and suddenly I was falling. Nothing but air under my skis. I hit with a jarring thud, but I was upright. Adrenaline flushed my veins, and I was giddy. I made it. Judd whooped and hollered. "Great job. I knew you could do it."

The next week, we approached a narrow chute. I always avoided those, but I found myself standing at the top, only my tips and tails making contact over the concave chute. I would rather have been just about anywhere than staring down the throat of this chute. I bounced gently. Still holding.

"OK, now tip the edge of your uphill ski to release. Make sure you're forward on your skis and be ready to make that first turn."

Yeah, right. Every nerve screamed at me to climb up the mountain to safety. Or stay here until a helicopter came with a long line to magically pluck me off the mountain. That wasn't going to happen, so I had to figure this out.

"And don't hug the mountain," Judd shouted from below. There was no room for error, but the exit was full of snow, no rocks. What was the worst that could happen? I tipped, my ski shot forward, and I whipped it around. Whew, made the first turn. Whoops, the second turn was coming up fast. I wrenched my ski around awkwardly, not the prettiest turn I'd ever made, but I was skiing, not tumbling down the mountain. The tension released, I swooped down the widening chute, making turn after turn with a huge smile on my face. I was ecstatic the first time I danced down a slalom course with quick, precise, short-radius turns without taking out a gate or a knee. I was talked off a cliff more than once, but Judd didn't give up. And every time, he was proved right—I could do it. The better I got, the more I knew I could do things I would never have imagined.

Eliane's passion for skiing was insatiable, and I wasn't far behind. It didn't take much for her to convince me to extend our season by joining another advanced ski camp in late spring at Mt. Bachelor in Oregon. At a pre-camp meeting in Bend, we met Steve, who lived in Tahoe. Upon meeting us, he spoke slowly and deliberately.

"Very nice to meet you. Where are you from?"

"We're from San Francisco, but we ski in Tahoe. We know Judd and Cliff from the Advanced Ski Clinics at Squaw Valley," Eliane responded in her usual fast clip, since I was stuck in my head trying to figure out how to answer the simple question. San Francisco? California? US? Where was I born or where do I live now? Lived all over the world? It's complicated—how much time do you have? Was he looking for the short answer or the long answer? Too soon to go into the details? After she said San Francisco, I got the cue that the short answer was best.

"Oh, you speak English!" I wasn't expecting that response. Why did he look so puzzled?

"Why wouldn't we speak English?" I asked.

"Uh, your names . . . sounded foreign. I thought maybe you were from Europe." That was a first, but we all laughed and learned how to ski in sticky spring snow, go faster in the gates, and navigate on a huge conical mountain where it was easy to get disoriented on the ever-widening base.

Back at the hospital, I sat in my manager's office. "You've really embraced our new challenge, ramping up to open the first bone marrow transplant center in the Bay Area."

"I love it. The science is fascinating, and I want to learn everything I can. It offers so much hope and promise for our patients."

"I'd like to offer you the position of Bone Marrow Transplant Coordinator. You'll be perfect in the role, and it will give you a chance to expand your skills beyond bedside nursing." Stunned, I sat back in my chair, speechless. I shouldn't have been, since I had interviewed for the position, but I had no experience in the subspecialty. Bedside nursing was all I knew. Being responsible for educating nurses and patients and supporting the new team of physicians and laboratory techs coming out from Texas to set up the program would be as much of a stretch as the ski clinic was. Fear gripped me, and I had that familiar feeling of standing over a precipice. Work skills were so different from skiing skills that it felt silly to compare. Or were they so different? I took the leap, leaning into the challenge. It worked. I thrived in the role, which set the foundation for the next phase in my career. When I thought about my plan to work overseas, the timing didn't seem right, and that goal receded.

By the time I added a master's in business administration in health services management to my quiver of diplomas, I was done with school. A switch turned off, and my love of academics waned. I wanted to *do* not learn. My formal education completed, I advanced into management roles with increasing responsibilities, had a solid group of girlfriends, was passionate about skiing in the winter, and took up running in the summer. Yet there was something missing. Nibbling around the edges of this whirlwind social life was a growing dissatisfaction with my love life. All those degrees and fun times meant nothing without intimacy. A two-year pattern of romantic relationships was leaving me feeling empty inside.

THERAPY

"I think I need a therapist," I said to Kim shortly after I got my master's degree. It was 1990, the start of a new decade, and I was ready for a change. Like Elizabeth, who had become an attorney, Kim had moved on from bedside nursing, pursuing a career in counseling.

Without missing a beat or probing the reason why, she said, "I have just the person for you." It was as if she had prepared a gift, wrapped it in luxurious paper with a fancy bow, and was waiting for the right moment to present it.

A few weeks later, I sat in front of Sarah, a kindly-looking woman with soft eyes, the beginning of crinkle lines, long blonde hair framing her kind face. I was instantly comfortable with her.

"I want to know why I can't seem to stay in a relationship for more than two years and why the men I end up with don't last. My childhood was great, so we don't need to talk about that—no issues, there. I have lots of friends and a satisfying job, so I just want to focus on this one thing—maybe two or three visits." To her credit, she didn't blink when I laid bare my spectacular lack of self-awareness.

"Tell me about your relationships. Are you in one now?" she said, displaying her skill in meeting me where I was.

I described my current relationship with Judd, the ski instructor who was fun but didn't seem to have much ambition, and my dilemma about Steve, the guy from the ski camp in Oregon, whom I had gotten closer to over the last two years skiing together in Tahoe. He was a few inches taller than me, with baby blue eyes, graying brown hair, and a trim moustache. When we were skiing, usually with Eliane and a group, we always let him go first, not wanting to be in front of him. His confidence on the slopes outstripped his skill, and he often snowballed down the mountain while we followed along, picking up his discarded skis and poles. However, I wasn't sure he was interested in the same things I was outside of skiing. I wanted a daring life with lots of travel and excitement and he seemed too normal, too stable with a good job and homeownership. That sounded boring, not adventurous. Could he be a compatible companion? She listened and gave me homework and topics to think about.

During the next session, she said, "I know you don't want to delve deeply into your childhood, but it would help me to know just a little. Would you be willing to share a few things about your parents and how you grew up?"

That seemed like a reasonable request. As I recited my life history like a well-worn track on a favorite album, her eyes widened. As my words piled higher and higher, I faltered. I had recounted the sequence of events involving all the moves, wars, and schools so many times that it had lost meaning to me, but somehow, in this room, with this person, the words landed differently. It was as though they piled up so high that they tumbled off a cliff and landed on the floor with a thud. By the time I got to the war in Bangladesh, my life sounded preposterous, even to me. When I finished, there was a moment of silence. She often took a few minutes to gather her thoughts and wasn't prone to exaggeration, so I waited. I didn't even need her to respond to know how absurd my opening statement had been in the first session. Maybe my childhood did deserve some scrutiny.

"You've had an unusual childhood. I wonder if you'd be open to exploring some themes that came up for me as I heard your story."

"Yes. I take back everything I said. I can talk about whatever you think is best. That was silly of me to say my childhood didn't matter." My cheeks burned with embarrassment, but she didn't laugh or admonish me.

"We're out of time for today, but I'd like to give you some homework." She went to her bookcase and scanned a couple of shelves before pulling a worn paperback out. "Take this book and try to read it before our next session."

I looked at the book's cover and read the title, *Too Scared to Cry*. The author was Lenore Terr, MD. "That's an interesting title."

"It's about the Chowchilla kidnapping, when twenty-six children were abducted in 1976. Remember that story? The title is a quote from one of the boys who received counseling."

"They were buried in a bus, right? I'll read it, but I never had anything that traumatic happen."

"It was a truck, but just keep an open mind."

In my apartment, I stared at the page, my vision blurring, my heart racing. I couldn't breathe. Reading about the Chowchilla children, trapped in a buried truck for sixteen hours, not knowing if they were going to live or die was riveting. Speeding through stories of other children the author described, I learned about children who suffered childhood traumas in the form of sexual abuse, some who had watched a parent being murdered, those who'd been abducted by a parent, and others who had been beaten. Since I hadn't gone through nearly the extremes that they had, I rejected the hypothesis that I was like them. However, I couldn't ignore how much the description of their reactions, statements, and behaviors mimicked mine. They reported freezing, numbness, temper tantrums, and submissive behaviors followed by a frenzied emotional storm, not at the time of trauma, but afterwards. During or immediately after, children often looked serious and immobile but didn't exhibit extreme verbal or physical actions. There were few tears and no screaming or loss of control. The title of the book was taken from a quote from one of the kidnapped children, "I was too scared to cry." Had I suffered childhood trauma and didn't know it? Were my seemingly unrelated behaviors linked to some events when growing up? I considered the possibilities. It would be hard to examine the contours of my background and think anything except it was an exceptionally privileged lifestyle full of travel, culture, and loving parents who did the best they could within the framework of parenting of the times. They assumed I was resilient, and I'd adapt no matter where we went. And I did. Didn't I? We loved living overseas. That was part of our family lore. The hard times were just part of the adventure.

I kept reading. There was the girl who knocked her two front teeth out, just like I did. It was undeniable. The examples of childhood trauma weren't always newsworthy. Sometimes the trauma was not extreme. Maybe when many small traumas stack up over time, it can have an outsized effect. I considered all the goodbyes never spoken, the friends I left behind, never to see again, the houses we thought we would return to but never did, the intense fear I had experienced in the war, being separated from dad when he was in danger, and all the uncomfortable first days of school. Maybe these all added up to something. The freezing, the rages, the numbness when I felt threatened, the desire for connection competing with the feeling of separateness—maybe these weren't normal. I thought about the repetitive nightmares I had about Mom being carried off on a train, like when the door almost closed in Japan with me on the platform when I was four. In the dream, the door slams shut, and Mom is carried away, leaving me there alone, crying. I needed to know more, and the next therapy session was different.

"I read the book. It's possible events in my childhood might affect my behavior now, but I don't understand why." I was ready to learn.

Sarah observed I expressed no anger over the traumas and losses and even made excuses for people. That seemed normal to me. After all, I couldn't blame Mom or Dad; it wasn't their fault.

"What about the man on the ship?" she asked.

"Maybe he was lonely. He was so nice to me."

She educated me about the ways predatory men groom children to gain their trust—a chilling thought. Ugh, his solicitous behavior now made a new kind of sense to me. She helped me see that the rage that popped up at unexpected times might be rooted in emotions I had suppressed. She even wondered if there could be a connection between the emotional trauma and all the injuries and illnesses I experienced in Peru and elsewhere, though that was a more tenuous conjecture. Even suggesting that was a possibility was a revelation that got me thinking.

Sarah also said that the way I minimized my trauma didn't change the impact it had on me, no matter how much I tried to deny its importance. Trauma was trauma, no matter how I tried to diminish it. My outsized reactions to seemingly random situations, such as the temper tantrums when I was eight, could be a displaced response.

It was a lot to process, and my head spun after every session as I sorted through, turned over, re-examined, and considered different parts of my childhood. I started to see how my overseas life was unusual and instead of being embarrassed about having imaginary friends in childhood, blown piano recitals, bad grades in college, emotional outbursts, and becoming numb under stress, I could accept that these were coping strategies I had developed. Some strategies were better than others with some fallout when the tactics weren't adequate for the situation or didn't allow me to grow.

In nursing school, I had learned about the fight-or-flight response, where the sympathetic nervous system is triggered by a frightening event to prepare the body to fight or flee. Adrenaline is released that causes a rapid heart rate, racing thoughts, and sweaty palms. Through Sarah, I learned a new term had been added by psychologists—freezing. Children can experience emotions that outstrip their ability to fight or run, and when there is no other option, emotional numbness can be protective. However, for the adult me, numbness could be a barrier to development. Freezing was part of the same process as my rages, except all the excess energy was compressed like a black hole instead of exploding like a bomb, Sarah explained.

When I felt emotionally threatened, I'd freeze and wasn't able to share my thoughts or needs. In fact, I stopped participating at all. That's a fast way to shut down communication in a conversation. Could that be behind the stalled relationships I was experiencing? I didn't know how to fight that response because when it happened, it was like a cold shroud dropping over me that I didn't have control over.

Sarah taught me strategies for catching early signs before I closed down, but first she had me do an inventory of small and large traumas I had experienced so I could understand the magnitude of them. The list was long. Then we worked on identifying early signs of a shut-down, such as a narrowing of my vision and the sensation of a shell encasing me when I was on my way to the raisin state. If I could stop those doors from closing, I could keep communication open. I could even let the other person know what I was feeling and ask for what I needed. That was harder. I learned to ask for time to regroup in situations where I needed it to allow some breathing room if I started feeling trapped. I developed an internal dialog when I'd lock down. I'd repeat the words, "Stay open, stay open." It was exhausting at first. Gradually, it became easier to halt the process.

"After making my list, I wonder why I'm not more messed up, like some of the kids who had bigger emotional issues in that book," I said.

"It's important to recognize how small and large traumatic episodes can build up, but you also seemed to have some key figures who offered support—your parents. While they might not have been perfect, they tried to keep you safe, while Sister Angelica, your Aunt Carol, and various friends along the way also helped. Sometimes all it takes is one person to make a difference." I sorted through all the positives I could think of and saw how they balanced the hard times. I had seen enough to know that every family has difficulties, no matter how much money they have or how lavish their lifestyle compared to mine. And even though I was more fortunate than many of the people I had to leave behind, the losses still hurt me.

Sarah showed me that my narrative around adventure and excitement could also include a stable romantic partner and home life and that there could be strength in steadiness. In my conversations with Steve, nothing I threw at him drove him away, even when I said I didn't know if I wanted children, that I wanted to travel to places unfamiliar to him, and that I might move to Seattle for a new job opportunity. His responses were that he wasn't sure about children either, he'd love to explore Asia or anywhere in the world, he was ready for a change and Seattle sounded interesting.

The beginning of the romantic phase of our relationship wasn't clean—we were both in relationships we had to end, and I held him at arm's length until we were disentangled. We started our life together in Seattle with new jobs, new mountain bikes, new maps, and new horizons in the far north. I was nervous about the commitment. I had doubts of being in a relationship for more than two years but took the plunge when he proposed. When Dad gave us the precious set of china with the hand-painted blue flowers from Denmark that he had selected for his parents, now long deceased, I knew this was serious business.

Steve was steady and calm, and it turned out that wasn't boring. Instead, he provided a solid foundation for our partnership, which eventually grew into a strong, flexible springboard for taking chances. Who knew all that could be in one package? He was also loyal, steadfast, knew all my secrets, and was unfailing in his support.

When we were unpacking in our new house in Seattle, I found the box labeled "Chuz."

"What's Chuz?" Steve asked.

"She's my doll from childhood," I said, pulling out a bedraggled Chuz, with her faded dress, matted hair, and sticky, peeling skin on her aging rubber limbs. Her blue eyes were still calm and steadfast, opening and closing as I tilted her back and forth. "She's really a mess. At some point, I should probably let go and throw her out."

"No way! If you've been hauling her around all these years, she must mean something to you. She had to have been an important part of your childhood. Chuz stays."

I stroked her tangled hair and touched her thick black eyelashes. My fingers slid over the familiar dimples on her plump elbow as I cradled her. I remembered the black-and-white photograph of her in my crib, how she dangled from my hand on the train tracks in Japan and sat on my lap in the cargo plane when we were evacuated from Lahore. How she went round and round the world with me, the one constant in my life who was still there, always ready. Steve was right. She had to stay.

Steve and I became expert skiers in the shadow of Mt. Rainier, got speedier when coached by an Olympic ski racer on the perpetual snows of Blackcomb Glacier, mountain biked through miles of sun dappled cedar forests in British Columbia, paddled 450 miles on the Yukon River in a canoe, tested my fear of heights by rock climbing with ropes and harnesses, sampled scuba diving in the Great Barrier Reef, and decided we had too many expensive hobbies. At forty-five, I wondered about backpacking. He sighed, saying we finally had enough money for nice hotels, but donned his pack and enthusiastically joined me on a mad dash to high alpine long-distance trails around the world before we got too old. We hiked several-hundred-mile wilderness trails in the Sierra Nevada, Andes, Alps, and Alaska, and met many retired trekkers who inspired us. We weren't too old for adventure—we were just getting started. I wanted to share what I had learned and connect people to nature, becoming a hike leader at a local state park and a Sierra Club backpack leader.

It took five visits to Alaska and the Yukon before we saw the northern lights. But it wasn't my first time. As soon as the sky lit up with shimmering curtains of green light, I remembered seeing them in Denmark with my parents when we had been on home leave from Pakistan. It felt good to share this extraordinary experience with Steve.

Five months of traipsing through Hong Kong, Vietnam, Laos, Cambodia, Thailand, Singapore, and Indonesia, where Steve stopped to eat every single morsel of street food he passed, convinced me I had the right companion. Finally, I had the life I always dreamed of and the sense of belonging I craved. It wasn't a physical place. It was wherever we were. Finally, I was home.

EPILOGUE

Untethered

MOM

Mom's right hand gripped mine as she, wild-eyed, locked me in her gaze. Tears streamed down my face as I looked back at her, unwavering, helpless to do anything but murmur, "I'm here, Mom, you're safe." It was a lie. I couldn't keep her safe. Her brain clashed in mortal combat with the massive stroke that had nearly slayed her a few hours earlier. It wasn't clear what the outcome would be. I couldn't protect her, but I was at her side in intensive care, trying to force healing powers through her eyes, the portals to her soul.

My gaze slid to Elizabeth, who was holding Mom's limp, flaccid left hand. Elizabeth looked back at me, entire volumes of emotion sliding wordlessly between us, sloshing back and forth, our shared nursing experience with mortality stalling the usual platitudes about miracles and faith. Elizabeth whispered to Mom to breathe in and out, iiiin and ouuut. She stroked Mom's temples gently, drawing small circles on her skin like a phosphorescent radar blip. I looked at her in wonder that she knew the exact right thing to do. Slowly, the high voltage energy in the room dissipated, dissolving into the soft, rhythmic breathing Elizabeth was modeling. We spoke in hushed tones, not saying much of anything, just being. Waiting. Waiting for what? The acrid odor of alcohol and antiseptic saturated the air and beeps from the IV pump punctuated the landscape at irregular intervals. Time stood still.

Suddenly, Mom clenched my hand with the strength of Hercules, my arm shooting out as she straightened hers. Then she jerked our clasped hands to her chest like a tightly wound spring; her torso arched off the bed. A deep guttural sound flew out of her mouth as she fell back. Monitor alarms screeched insistently. She was motionless.

"What happened?" I cried, leaping from the chair, my hand still in Mom's clutches. Elizabeth glanced up at the monitor, then back at me, not saying a word.

"What is happening? Is that it? Please tell me."

She stared at me with a look of profound sadness. I didn't want to ask, but I had to. "What are you seeing on the monitor?" Elizabeth had turned the monitor away from me earlier so I wouldn't stare at the crazy EKG lines tracing across the screen in luminous green script. Her hand made a horizontal slicing movement across her throat, an obvious flat-line reference.

I screamed a silent *nooooooooooooooo*, it's too soon, we're not done, we have more adventures, I'm not ready. No sound came out. My mind went numb, filled with thick cotton, and the world turned black. *You were always there for me. You can't be gone.*

Elizabeth's arms hugged me as the intensive care team assembled in a semi-circle at the foot of the bed, summoned by their master, the monitor. Their subdued countenance contrasted with the frenetic activity before we made her a no-code, when her heart rhythm was streaking across the monitor in a demented etch-a-sketch pattern and the intensivist was barking medication orders in a futile attempt to change the inevitable outcome. Mom had never wanted extraordinary measures taken if things looked bad and they had looked very bad indeed. Elizabeth shooed everyone out of the room, and I sank down in my chair, holding Mom's hand, still warm from the life she had lived, wondering if I had made the right decision.

I was exhausted from the exercise of deciding her code status. The ER doctor had sent me to her house to retrieve her Advance Directive documents where she clearly indicated she didn't want to be kept alive artificially. Because she had listed Dad as her agent to make health care decisions, he wouldn't accept her wishes without his authorization. I couldn't make him understand that Dad was too medically fragile to travel and too hard of hearing to talk on the telephone and he kept her a full code. When Mom was transferred to the ICU, the doctor and nurses there were very concerned about her erratic heart rhythm and spoke to me in somber tones about how precarious her condition was. They wondered why I wanted her to be a full code. Breaking down in tears, I sobbed that despite my grief, I was a nurse and could make the hard decisions, but that the ER doctor overrode me. The ICU doctor called the ER doctor and after a stern exchange, they allowed me to make the final decision to make her a no code. It was the right thing to do. But nothing felt right about the situation.

Elizabeth was with me because an hour before, the nurses had been pestering me about not being alone, seeing in their crystal ball that the situation was dire. I kept telling them Steve would be here in an hour or two, but they weren't satisfied.

"Don't you have anyone closer? Please make the call. Or I'll call for you," said the nurse. That seemed unnecessarily dramatic. She wasn't asking; she was demanding. As she left Mom's room to care for other patients, I promised I would call. I dialed Elizabeth's number. It was 2019, and we had been friends for nearly forty of my sixty-three years. She lived only ten minutes from the hospital. No answer. The nurse wasn't giving up, though. When she returned to check on Mom, I preempted her question and said, "No answer. I'll call her again." This time, Elizabeth answered on the first ring.

"What's up? I was on a call with a client." Her voice was crisp and professional, in work mode.

"Um, uh, well, Mom's in the hospital. It looks like it might be serious. I was wondering if it wouldn't be too much trouble … maybe … "

"I'll be right there. Give me ten minutes." Her voice softened.

"Are you sure you're not bus—"

"Shhh, shhh, shhh, no more talk. I'll be there in a flash." She hung up. My heart overflowed with love for this person who would drop anything to comfort me. I thought of Kim, an hour away, and Cindy, a flight away, and Eliane, on the other side of the bay. I knew any of them would have done the same thing, as I would have for them. Over the years, we had always pulled together for the crises and tragedies, as much as we had celebrated the joys of unions, births, and achievements over a lifetime.

Now Elizabeth and I sat there, stunned. There was nothing to be done but wait for Steve, and I couldn't let go of Mom's hand. I sat there confounded, almost able to pretend she was still living. Mom couldn't be gone because Dad was still alive. He was ninety-five; she was eighty-six. He had to die first. It was logical that the frail, older parent would die first. He was so frail; she was so strong. He was practically bedbound; she had just returned from a solo trip to a remote area of the Yucatan, ever the adventurer. Our plans centered on the understanding that he'd pass on first and then Mom and I would travel again, like we always had, only we'd have Steve with us. There was no room for this preposterous scenario. It was so absurd no one had even voiced it.

I heard Elizabeth talking to Cindy, her responses telling me that Cindy was scheduling her flight. Kim was next, and texts buzzed on my phone. I couldn't respond yet, but I felt the love.

Steve walked in and gasped when he saw Mom's face, already looking waxy and plastic, her hand still in mine. She had slipped away, despite my holding her tight, trying to keep her close, keep her safe, keep her here. My recurring nightmare had finally come true, where she was carried away on her last journey down that track to the other side … and I hadn't been able to stop it. He hugged me and I clung to him for a long time.

By the time we left the hospital, I felt a kind of anesthetized peace, more of a void than true harmony. How incredible is the human spirit that within hours we can adapt to the awfulness of such loss? Or maybe I was in shock.

"Oh, no, I still have to tell Dad," I said, as we prepared to leave the room. There was a precipitous realization that more distress was to come. Weak, frail Dad, who had been housebound in their dream Sausalito home, where Mom cared for him with minimal help, still not wanting people underfoot. He was still waiting to hear if she was okay.

When I pulled into the garage, I took a deep breath. I would have given anything to be somewhere else, to not have to do this next task. I opened the door from the garage to the kitchen, walked into the dining room with the carved wooden figures sprouting human hair from Irian Jaya and proceeded to the living room with the colorful expressionist paintings evoking a cockfight and market scene in Bali, the black hand-tooled leather-clad coffee table from Peru and the bronze camels in descending size from Pakistan. The twinkling lights from the nearby hill and dark space of Richardson Bay did not penetrate my consciousness as I made my way down the soft Persian runner in the hallway.

Dad looked so small in his bed when I walked into his large bedroom, his six-foot frame diminished by age and chronic disease, surrounded by framed cases of the arrowheads he collected when he was a robust football player in his prime.

Ever stoic, he immediately said, "Well, is it good news or bad news?"

"Not good news," I said. I went to him and took his hand. I had to get the unspeakable words out as fast as I could. "I'm so sorry, but Mom didn't make it."

"Oh no," he said. I raced through the recitation.

"Mom had a stroke, and it was a bad one. We did everything we could, but she didn't make it."

"Oh, no. Oh, no."

"I was there when she died, holding her hand. I told her you loved her."

"Oh, no. Oh, no. Oh, no."

Later he asked, "Were you there?"

"Yes, Dad, I was there, holding her hand." Over the next two days, he asked me over and over if I was there when she died. I understood why. He wanted to make sure she wasn't alone. The horror was inconceivable to us both, and it was impossible to absorb.

DAD

Mom's absence was a huge rent in the fabric of our lives. For six months, I stayed with Dad in the Sausalito house because I couldn't figure out what else to do. Steve came back and forth, an hour each way, holding things together at our house, until one day he asked, "Are you ever coming home?" Of course, I was coming home. When? I had no answer.

Every day felt like walking through molasses as I went through my ever-expanding checklist of things to do. Arrange Dad's medical appointments. Call financial institutions. Call them again. Talk to lawyers. Sign papers. Sign more papers. Visit the notary. Make grocery lists. Make dinner, endless dinners, a river of dinners I couldn't taste. I was numb with grief and had constant low-level anxiety over managing the endless details of Dad's life. And now, added to the list: Move home. But how? I went in circles. Hire more help? Move him in with us? Send him to assisted living?

Every night when I kissed him goodnight, he asked, "Did you check the doors?"

"Yes, Dad, the garage door is down, the front door is locked, and all the windows are closed." If I had forgotten to check, I'd immediately do a perimeter patrol, just as he had done for me throughout my childhood.

"Good, good," he said as he nestled into his pillow, safely tucked in for the night. Unless the nightmares came.

Some mornings, when I asked how his night was, he responded, "Not good, they were coming to get me again."

"Who?"

"I don't know. They're always coming to get me. Sometimes they get close. They almost got me this time."

Who were these demons chasing him in the night? Were they the Japanese from World War II when he was stationed in the South Pacific? Or Pakistan? Or Bangladesh?

Sometimes I heard him call out in the night. I'd rush into his bedroom to find him quaking in his bed, his sheets pulled up to his chin, pale blue eyes wide with fright.

"You're safe, Dad. I'm here." I would pat his hand and sit with him until his breathing calmed. It was all I could offer, knowing I couldn't be where he needed me most, inside his head.

Eventually, Dad announced his decision in his usual pragmatic way. He would move into an assisted living facility, and I would do all the research and bring him the information so we could decide which one. After finding him a suitable place near our house in Kenwood, Steve and I helped him make his last move. The facility was built around large interior courtyards with some rooms facing the street and others facing the courtyard. His only request was that he have a ground-floor apartment on the inside with no exterior doors or windows to the street, always mindful of safety. He worried about break-ins through an outside opening and navigating stairs in a fire or earthquake if the elevator was broken. My best friend, Cindy, ever present in those months by phone and with frequent visits, flew up to help, bringing a much-needed lightness to the grim task.

It was all very pleasant at Dad's new place, with his first-floor apartment looking out into the secure manicured gardens of the courtyard, a dining room with decent food, caring staff, and a spacious two-room apartment with a full kitchen. I visited nearly every day, prepared his favorite foods, took him on walks through the courtyard, and managed his affairs. But it wasn't the same as home, when Mom took care of everything. Every day was tinged with sadness and with each season came additional losses of independence. His world narrowed to his bed and an endless cycle of TV shows: *McHale's Navy, MASH, Star Trek, Andy Griffith, Three Stooges*, and *Laurel and Hardy* all brought him back to the time when he was in his prime and the world was less complicated. The weekday shows were just to pass the time, leading up to the big event every Saturday night, the one where I made sure to have a special meal and a thimble of wine for him—*Columbo*. Dad knew every episode and would tell me in advance who did it and how Columbo was going to figure it out, and he still loved every minute of it.

Between Mom's death and the old-time TV shows was a precious gift, the gift of time. Mom had been so full of energy and vitality that she dominated our little family. Without her, Dad and I had many quiet conversations that might never have happened. He spun endless tales of riding the rails with his brother Leonard during the Great Depression and sailing on the PT boats as a gunner in the Navy in Papua New Guinea, Borneo, and the Philippines during World War II. I surreptitiously dragged my notebook out of the bedside stand and scribbled notes. I dragged the dogeared world atlas out daily as he remembered place names where he fought the Japanese, met General MacArthur, and ate disagreeable canned Australian rabbit when supply lines were disrupted. He could still reel off names of the big battles: Milne Bay, Wake Island, Mindoro and more. From their PT boats, they patrolled rivers deep in the jungles of Borneo, bucked fifty-foot swells in the Sulu Sea in the Philippines, and stared down Papua New Guinea tribesmen in full war paint in a canoe. Somewhere in the tangle of islands, the demons of his nightmares must have originated.

After the war, he had planned to return to Kansas, to continue farming near his family, but a medic changed everything. When Dad was stuck in a military hospital with malaria in the Philippines, this medic stayed up late at night talking to Dad about the new GI Bill and developing a roadmap for his future. He cross-examined Dad about his interests, picked out a field of study, and directed him to apply to Colorado State University. Dad laughed and thought it was a game. After a hot, dusty summer plowing fields after the war, he realized his world had been cracked open, and the farm wasn't going to be enough. He followed the medic's road map, enrolled at Colorado State, and graduated with a bachelor's degree in Agronomy, the study of soil science, water hydrology, and crop production—a perfect fit for a farmer's son.

He could have stayed in his first safe engineering job with the USDA in Colorado as a soil scientist, but fate intervened. While perusing announcements on the company bulletin board, he spotted a tiny vague notice about a soils engineering job overseas for single applicants only, without naming the country or any details. He located a typewriter and wrote a letter, inquiring about the position and describing his qualifications. He heard nothing for weeks. One day, a large envelope arrived containing airline tickets to Afghanistan and instructions for picking up a passport. He disembarked in New York, found his contact, and took the passport that was handed to him. His journey continued to Karachi, West Pakistan by air, then by train to Quetta, West Pakistan and by car to Kabul, Afghanistan. He had been seeking adventure, and he found it, meeting engineers and consultants on the dusty job site in the Helmand Valley who would link him to other international engineering jobs for decades.

When I packed Dad's belongings in Sausalito, I found a book tucked into the back corner of his closet. A book thick with yellowing pages and a hard black cover, it was hefty enough that still having it after seventy years had to have been a deliberate choice after all our moves. The title, *The Royal Road to Romance*, was intriguing. Published in 1925, it had dad's name and "Lucas, KS" written on the first page. I brought it to Dad, asking him if he remembered this book. He reached out with his thin, bony hand lined with protruding blue veins and had a soft look on his face.

"Ah, yes, this was the first book I ever bought with my own money, right after high school." I read the book cover to cover, tracing the adventures of an intrepid young man, Richard Halliburton, who traveled around the world through Europe, the Middle East, India, and Asia, not unlike the path of Dad's career. It was filled with quirky anecdotes of a swaggering adventurer that had to have lit Dad's imagination just as he was setting out on his own first overseas adventure in the war.

I wondered if Halliburton's Alhambra story led to Dad's fateful choice to visit the storied place on his first vacation from Afghanistan. He met Mom under the spell of that magical palace in Spain and proposed months later. It was pure kismet.

In the last few weeks of Dad's life, his once razor-sharp mind finally started to slip. It started with his announcement that he had a job offer in Jakarta, then transitioned to Peru, where he was frantic to get a feasibility study done so he didn't get in trouble with his boss. That theme played out over many days.

One day, while we were watching *McHale's Navy*, he said, "I think we're going to be separated soon."

He must be trying to tell me something and the end must be near, I thought sadly. I took his hand in mine. "Why do you say that?"

"I just feel it. Try to get to Karachi if you can. I'll be going out on the southern route to Kandahar. You take the arrowheads and go a different way, through Peshawar. We'll try to meet up in Quetta."

Oh dear, I thought, *now he's in Afghanistan*.

A week later, he called me at home, complaining that the caregivers wouldn't help him get to San Francisco.

"I'll be there in an hour, but you don't need to go to San Francisco," I said.

"You don't know everything."

"I know that I make your appointments, and you don't see Dr. Jacobson anymore. I have all your doctors come to you now. Besides, it's Saturday."

"This isn't a doctor. It's . . . it's people you don't know."

"Who? I can't help you if I don't know where you're going."

"I have to meet people from the government. They expect me to show up." I sat bolt upright. Was he so confused that he was making up fiction? All his other episodes were based on his life, where he was back in Peru worrying about a report, or getting out of Afghanistan, or in Halmahera Island on the PT boats. Or did he have a secret life I didn't know about? Could he have been a spy? It was ludicrous. Or was it? Maybe he was a very good spy. I held my tongue, hoping he'd say more, but he went silent and by the time I got there, he had come back to the present.

A week later, just shy of his ninety-eighth birthday, he slipped away in his sleep, drawing his last breath by himself in the quiet of the night. Any secrets he had, he took to the grave. There was no drama, no agony, no nothing, just an absence of life where there had been a thin thread of being. He died the way he lived, quiet, steady, and unobtrusive, while Mom went out in a fiery ball, just the way she lived.

I was left with the crushing realization that there was no one left who shared my childhood memories, no one to say, "Remember when ... " No one but Chuz, whose matted hair and peeling plastic skin reminded me of a lifetime of adventure. All I had left were my precious notes from Dad, Mom's travel articles, Chuz, and my own memories. Perhaps I should write them down, I mused.

AFTERWORD

Deciphering my family's history required quite a bit of sleuthing. Sparse clues and nostalgic fragments spurred me on, despite the roadblocks. I analyzed many immigration stamps in our passports, squinted at a small collection of photographs, and read every page of the only two yearbooks I had—one from my first year of school in Lahore and one from my last year of high school in Marin. There were years with a few photos, but no report cards, no teacher's notes, no school papers. Only fuzzy memories of hasty military evacuations, temporary ceasefires, and wrenching goodbyes. How could I find someone who remembered?

Bangladesh was particularly void of mementos. I idly poked at my keyboard one day, entering Dhaka American School, Dacca American School, and Dacca International School. Nothing. I gave up, hoping something tangible would surface as I went through Mom's and Dad's possessions. A few days later, I added "1960" to the search string and a single image of a bland library interior appeared. It didn't look familiar, but a click landed me in the cryptically named "AISD Alumni Network" on Facebook. The letters did not elicit the slightest buzz of recognition. Once the acronym was decoded, I learned that the American International

School Dhaka was the name of the new school, opened after the war, after my classmates were scattered to the winds. The images of shiny modern buildings and well-maintained fields on a spacious campus bore no resemblance to the humble residence that housed the school in my memory. It was another dead end.

Later, I scanned posts in the AISD group filled with photos of recent events and unfamiliar buildings. Until four letters leaped off the screen—DASS. A flash of memory and my nerves buzzed—the trail was warm again. That was my school, the Dacca American Society School. The edges of the words became fuzzy as my mind raced to take it all in, like trying to eat a whole hamburger at once. The laconic paragraph left me hungry for more. I parsed each phrase, one at a time. "Seventh grade, school was in two houses, never had a library like the one pictured." Yes. The clues were coming together. I kept reading. "Quick evacuation because of the Liberation War." Rebecca had gone through the same traumatic time in the violent, chaotic, early days of the war when we were young girls. There were people who remembered, who were like me.

Time contracted. It was April 13, 1971, and I was at the airport in Dacca. I saw it all like it was yesterday: the inky black night, the plane coming in with dim lights, the Pakistani soldiers disembarking before they boarded us. The terror of leaving Dad behind in a violent conflict.

My heart sank when I saw the date of the post was three years ago. Had I missed an opportunity to connect with kindred classmates? I wrote a comment on the thread and sent a direct message to Rebecca. I checked my computer obsessively. Relief flooded through me when she responded, and I pressed her to meet with me. We arranged a call for the next day.

I felt a surge of electricity that jolted me into overdrive when Rebecca talked about Dacca the next day. Every nerve ending tingled. The words piled on so fast I could barely keep up, my brain trying to accommodate all the familiar words being spoken by a stranger, mirroring everything I went through, how we had to leave suddenly, our classrooms were in bedrooms in a house, she swam at the Intercontinental Hotel, made friends easily but had to leave so fast, how they evacuated to Tehran, and lived in a bunch of different countries. My life story streamed out of someone else's mouth. Our words tumbled over themselves like two streams coming together over a rocky weir, a gush of emotional intensity that neither of us was prepared for. It was astounding. It was thrilling. It was too much. I abruptly cut off the call, saying I wanted to stay in touch but had to go. I was on overload, unable to absorb more. She felt the same way, messaging me later that she wouldn't be able to continue communicating with me. It was too overwhelming for her.

Discouraged to lose the thread of connection, I took to my keyboard again. In my detective work, I kept stumbling across, and passing over, the term "Third Culture Kids" (TCKs). When I finally clicked on it, a new world was revealed. There I was, defined in one long sentence: "The first culture of third-culture kids refers to the culture of the country from which the parents originated (passport culture), the second culture refers to the culture in which the family currently resides (host culture), and the third culture refers to the distinct cultural ties among all third culture individuals that share no connection to the first two cultures." Third Culture Kid—an awkward phrase that said so much. I found solace in the book *Third Culture Kids, Growing Up Among Worlds,* discovering a network of people among the 220 million of more TCKs like me. A section of the book called "Finding Someone Who Remembers" nailed what I was seeking. The internet revealed a plethora of TCK social media groups, podcasts, and books. In one Facebook group, Third Culture Kids-TCKs Worldwide, I found many people who grew up in the same countries I did, with many of the same challenges adjusting to life in one place.

I learned of another Facebook Group, Alumni of D.A.S.S., that was specific to our cohort of students and faculty who had attended the old school. It was dazzling to hear from so many classmates. A flurry of posts resulted in images of yearbooks, Dacca street scenes, orientation pamphlets, and school badges. Best of all, one kind person posted photos of our school, including the backyard and basketball court, confirming that my fuzzy memory was more intact than I had thought.

To my relief, Rebecca circled back to me, and we went on to exchange book titles of treatises that aided in our understanding of the cultural and political forces that had swirled around us. Books such as *Blood Telegram: Nixon, Kissinger, and a Forgotten Genocide*, *The Cruel Birth of Bangladesh*, *Memoirs of an American Diplomat*, *The Last Guardian: Memoirs of Hatch Barnwell, ICS of Bengal*, and *Freedom at Midnight* helped me grasp the layers of history around British occupation, partition, and the civil war that led to the independence of Bangladesh.

Putting all the clues together and finding a community made me feel whole again. A place where I belonged.

Combining her enthusiasm for exploration with her compassion as an oncology nurse, Inga Aksamit pens award-winning narratives that bridge cultures and celebrate the human spirit. Her love of adventure has taken her around the world to hike in remote mountain ranges, explore ancient ruins, and establish deep connections to others.

She started traveling at age four when her family embraced the expat lifestyle and moved from Vacaville, California to Lahore, Pakistan for her father's work. Her childhood experiences as a third-culture kid (TCK) in Pakistan, Bangladesh, Peru, and Indonesia allow her to see the world through a multifaceted lens of empathy, wonder and discovery. Her hiking memoir, "Highs and Lows on the John Muir Trail," won The Best Outdoor Book award for 2015 from the Outdoor Writers Association of California and "The Hungry Spork Trail Recipes" won the Best Outdoor Guidebook award in 2020.

www.ingramcontent.com/pod-product-compliance
Lightning Source LLC
Chambersburg PA
CBHW020230130626
46549CB00005B/1811